A Concise Dictionary of
EGYPTIAN
ARCHAEOLOGY

M. Brodrick & A. A. Morton

SENATE

A Concise Dictionary of Egyptian Archaeology

First published in 1902 by Methuen & Company Ltd, London.

This edition first published in 1996 by Senate, an imprint of
Random House UK Ltd, Random House, 20 Vauxhall Bridge
Road, London SW1V 2SA.

ISBN 1 85958 486 1

Printed and bound in Guernsey by The Guernsey Press Co. Ltd

PREFACE

THIS little book has been prepared for publication with the idea of offering to students and to travellers in Egypt a handy book of reference, which contains in a condensed form information that would otherwise have to be sought for in various large volumes.

In illustrating the figures of the Egyptian gods the form most frequently represented on the monuments has in each case been chosen. It has not been possible, from want of space, to depict more than one aspect or one set of attributes.

A selection only of royal names has been inserted.

The system of transliteration adopted will be found under the heading "Hieroglyphs." In the case of particular names, where the Greek or some other form has become familiar to the general reader, the word has not been transliterated, but the more common spelling has been used, such as in Thothmes, Isis, and Serapis.

LIST OF ILLUSTRATIONS

A CONCISE DICTIONARY

OF

EGYPTIAN ARCHAEOLOGY

A

Aāḥ, who is purely a moon God, shares with Khensu and Thoth the emblems of the lunar crescent and solar disk. He is sometimes connected with Thoth (*q.v.*).

Aāḥ-ḥetep I.

Wife of Seqenen-Rā III., an obscure king of the end of Dynasty XVII. and mother of Aāḥmes I., first king of the XVIIIth Dynasty. In 1860, the diggers of M. Mariette discovered at Thebes the coffin of this queen, but M. Mariette being unfortunately absent at the time, the mummy was robbed of many valuable articles. The coffin cover is in the shape of a mummy, and is gilt from top to bottom. The articles found in the coffin included a double-hinged bracelet with gold figures, on a groundwork of blue enamel ;

Aāḥ.

a large bracelet opening with a hinge ; an axe with a handle of cedar-wood covered with gold-leaf and ornamented with lapis lazuli, carnelian and turquoise ; a dagger in a sheath of gold ; a gold chain with pendant scarabaeus ; a large gold collar with hawks' heads at each end, etc. These objects are now in the Cairo Museum.

Aāh-hetep II. She was the daughter of Queen Nefertári and Áāḥmes I., and wife of Ámen-ḥetep I. (Dynasty XVIII.).

Aāḥmes I. *Neb-peḥti-Rā.* First king of Dynasty

XVIII., cir. 1587 B.C. Nefert-ári was his queen, and he had by her six children. Áāḥmes began the great war of independence which resulted in the expulsion of the Hyksos. He captured their capital *Ḥat-uārt* (Tanis ?) and drove them into the Palestine desert. He then subjugated the Mentiu, or Bedawin. Turning south he went up the Nile to Semneh and repelled the Ethiopians. The body of Áāḥmes, in a fair state of preservation, is in the Cairo Museum. He appears to have died in the prime of life.

Aāḥmes se-Nit, *Khnem-àb-Rā,* Amāsis II., Dynasty

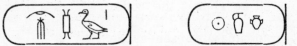

XXVI., B.C. 572-528. He married the princess Ānkhs-en-Rā-Nefert, daughter of Psammetichus II. This Pharaoh encouraged commercial enterprise by opening Naukratis (*q.v.*) to Greek traders both as a free port and as a place of settlement. He also conquered Cyprus, and made an alliance with Croesus, king of Lydia, in the hope of stemming the tide of Persian invasion.

Åalu, Fields of. In the legend of the "Destruction of Mankind," found in the tomb of Seti I. and elsewhere, we learn how that Rā, tired of ruling disobedient people on earth, retired to the sky. "His desire was fulfilled, and having reached the upper regions, he inspected the territory which he had there chosen for his own, declared his purpose of gathering many men about him in it, and created for their future accomodation the various divisions of the heavenly world. His majesty spake : ' Let there be set a great field,' and there appeared the Field of Rest ; ' I will gather plants in it,' and there appeared the Field of *Åaru* (Åalu), ' Therein do I gather as its inhabitants things which hang from heaven, even the stars ' " (Erman). It was to this part of the divine world that souls made their way on the death of the body. The " Book of the Dead " speaks of it as " the field which produced the divine harvests," which the blessed departed spent their time in harvesting. The barley here grew to seven cubits in height. The fields of Åalu were surrounded by a wall of iron, broken by several doors, and traversed by a river ; the ways which led to it were mysterious. The idea has been compared to the Greek Elysian fields.

Åāmu, or Āmu. The name given by the Egyptians to the Asiatic tribes inhabiting the Sinaitic Peninsula, who were probably Semites. They may be seen depicted upon the walls of the tomb of Khnem-ḥetep II. at Beni Hasan ; where they have a distinctly Semitic type of face, are coloured yellow, and wear the beard—forbidden to the Egyptians. Their clothes are of a shape and colour peculiar to themselves.

Aāni. The Egyptian name for the cynocephalus (*q.v.*).

Abbot. *See* PAPYRI.

Abydos. Greek name for *Abet*, capital of the eighth nome of Upper Egypt, site near the modern Girgeh.

Chief deity An-hur.   Seti I. and Ramses II. built fine
temples here.   Abydos was a burial place from time immemorial.   Petrie has found there the earliest known
royal tombs; they appear to belong to the Ist and IInd
Dynasties.   Tradition says that it was the burial place
of Osiris, and hence the custom of bringing the dead,
if not to be buried, at least to rest in the sacred precincts for a time.   (*See* THIS.)

Abydos, **Tablets of.**   One of these was discovered in
1818 by Bankes and given to the British Museum.   It
is much damaged.   The other was found by Dümichen
in 1864, and is still in the temple.   The first tablet
gives the names of the chief kings who reigned over
Egypt from Mena to Ramses II.   The second tablet,
which begins with Mena and ends with Seti I., gives
the names of seventy-five kings.   It is therefore not
a complete list, but it is valuable as giving the kings
in their right historical or chronological order.

Acacia.   There are now several kinds in Egypt, but
probably those mentioned on the monuments as *Shenti*
and *Ashu* were respectively the Arab "sont" tree, or
acacia Nilotica, and the *acacia Seyal*.   The flora of
Egypt being so limited, these were of immense importance as being almost the only trees affording wood for
carpentering purposes.   The wood was also used for
making statues.

Achoris.   A king of Dynasty XXIX., who according
to Diodorus Siculus, joined forces with the King of
Cyprus in an unfortunate campaign against Artaxerxes II.

Ādet.   One of the names of the solar bark.

Agriculture.   The extraordinary fertility of the soil
rendered agriculture in one sense an easy matter.
The land uncovered after the inundation would pro-

duce easily three or four successive crops. But a great amount of irrigation was necessary in order to bring the later crops to perfection. For this the *Shadoof* (*q.v.*) was largely used, and men also carried two pots attached to a yoke over the shoulders. The implements in use in ancient times were very much like those still used by the Fellâhin. The clumsy wooden plough was attached to the horns of a yoke of oxen. The hoes were of wood, with broad blades and short handles. The seed having been sown, it was then trampled into the stiff muddy soil by sheep being driven over it. The corn when ripe was cut with a small sickle, not near the earth, but just under the ears. The sickle is in most cases short-handled, slightly curved and made of wood, set with flint teeth, so that the process of reaping must have been one of sawing rather than cutting. As soon as the corn was cut, the tax collector came to gather the official tenth before the grain was stored. The " treading out the corn " was most frequently done by donkeys under the Old Empire, but later, oxen were usually employed. Barley and wheat are both represented on the monu ments, and occasionally a crop which is in all probability the modern *dhurra*. This crop was pulled up by the roots, and the heads separated from the stalks by a peculiar implement that looks like a comb. Vegetables must also have been extensively cultivated, since they figure so largely among the offerings. Vines and olive trees were also grown, the former being trained over trellises supported by forked poles. Certain papyri and tomb inscriptions give most doleful accounts of the hard life and miserable condition of the agricultural labourer. This poverty is not neces- sarily to be attributed to harsh treatment from their superiors, but rather to their own improvidence.

Âḥi. A form of HARPOCRATES (*q.v.*), son of Hathor

Akh-en-Âten. *See* KHU-EN-ÂTEN, and ÂMEN- HETEP IV.

Akhmîm. The Ȧpu of the Egyptians, Panopolis of the Greeks, and Shmin or Chmim of the Copts. It was famous in ancient days for its linen weavers and stone cutters. Nestorius died there in banishment. There is a very extensive necropolis, in which many interesting MSS. have been found—notably the fragment of the pseudo-gospel of Peter.

Alabaster was used a great deal by the Egyptians for statues, sarcophagi, and vases of many kinds. The chief quarries were at a place called *Hat Nub*. There is another quarry in the desert behind Dowadîyeh, on the east bank near Minieh. There is alabaster near Asyût, but it is not sufficiently compact to admit of being quarried for use.

Alphabet. *See* HIEROGLYPHS.

Altar. Although small altars or "tables of offerings" appear frequently in the pictures and wall decorations of temples and tombs, only two genuine altars have been as yet found. One is in a court on the north side of the upper court of the temple of Dêr el Bahri (Dynasty XVIII.), and is a large stone platform measuring about 16 ft. 5 ins. by 13 ft. 9 ins., and about 5 ft. 3 ins. high. There are steps up to it on the west side by which the priest mounted, and thus faced the east. This altar was discovered by M. Naville during his excavation of the temple. The other is an altar to the Sun erected at the northern end of the forecourt of the great Temple at Abu Simbel.

Āmām.

Āmām. The Egyptian name for what is usually called the "Devourer." A composite creature, part lioness, part hippopotamus, part crocodile, frequently depicted seated on a small pylon. She is figured in the pictures of the judgment before

Osiris in the "Book of the Dead," and on the walls at Dêr el Medineh. She is called "she who destroys the wicked," and it has been supposed by some that it was her function to devour those who could not stand the judgment test. But very little is known on this point.

Amāsis II. *See* ȦȦḤMES-SE-NIT.

Amber. Beads of amber have been found at Abydos in the VIth and XIIth Dynasty tombs. The nearest amber obtainable was from the Baltic, so that intercourse of some kind was possible with Europe in the earliest time, a fact which is further proved by the tin which we know the Egyptians obtained for alloying copper to make bronze.

Ȧmen. A god who is more frequently found in conjunction with Rā than alone. His name signifies "the hidden one." Of all the gods perhaps he was the one most universally worshipped, though almost always in conjunction with some other god. Thus he was fused with Rā, with Ȧmsu, or Khnemu. His original *rôle* probably was as a god of the dead, and in late times "much mystic philosophy was evolved out of his name." (*See* ȦMEN RĀ, ȦMSU.)

Ȧmen-em-ḥāt. A name borne by four kings of Dynasty XII., but not confined to the use of royalty. It originated probably in a war cry, "Amen to the front!" One of the finest tombs at Beni Hasan is that of an Ȧmen-em-ḥāt (variant Ȧmeni), "Great chief of the Oryx Nome," and " confidential friend of the king " (Usertsen I.). From the inscriptions we learn that he made expeditions with, or on behalf of, his royal master. One of these expeditions was against the black people of Cush, on the southern Egyptian frontier.

Under Mentu-ḥetep of Dynasty XI., another Ȧmen-em-ḥāt received orders to transport the king's sarcophagus and its cover from the quarry to the eternal resting-place of his lord.

Amen-em-ḥāt I., *Se-ḥetep-ab-Rā*, first king and

founder of Dynasty XII., cir. 2778-2748 B.C., probably
of Theban origin, and most likely a descendant of the
Amen-em-ḥāt (*q.v.*) who was a prince under Mentu-ḥetep,
of Dynasty XI. His wars of aggression in all quarters
have been recorded in rock inscriptions and papyri.
He and his successors are known as much for their
wise home government as for the glory of their victories
abroad. Something of the internal conditions of the
country may be learnt from the " Story of Se-Nehat."
The temple to Amen at Thebes was founded by
Amen-em-ḥāt I., and there he set up a red granite
portrait of himself. During the last ten years of his
reign he associated with him on the throne his young
son, Usertsen. It was for this son that he wrote the
" Precepts" contained in the Sallier Papyrus II. From
a papyrus of Berlin (" Les Papyrus de Berlin," par
M. Chabas) it would seem that there was some
mystery about his death.

Amen-em-ḥāt II., *Nub-Kau-Rā*, third king of Dyn-

asty XII., and Son of Usertsen I., with whom he shared
the throne for some years. He followed the example
of his predecessors in extending the southern boundary
of his possessions, building well-fortified places on the
frontier to protect the people from the incursions of
negroes. The region was important on account of its
gold and precious stones. An inscribed stone at
Abydos commemorates certain explorations in the
conquered country in search of the precious products.
One of these expeditions, led by a distinguished official
named Se-Hathor, penetrated beyond the Second

Cataract to the land of *He-ha*. At Tanis, a life-size black granite statue of Nefert, wife of Åmen-em-hāt, has been discovered. Besides the traces of his work at Arsinsoë (*see* "Hawara, Biahmu, and Arsinoë," Petrie), we have records at Karnak that he added some work to the temple begun there by his father. After reigning for twenty-nine years, Åmen-em-hāt associated his son Usertsen II. on the throne with him.

Åmen-em-hāt III., *Maāt-en-Rā*, cir. 2622-2578 B.C.,

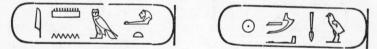

sixth king of Dynasty XII. Two daughters of this king are known, the princesses Ptah-neferu and Sebek-neferu. The pyramid of this king stands at Hawara, at the entrance to the Fayûm. It is built of brick, coated with limestone. The Labyrinth (*q.v.*) was the work of Åmen-em-hāt III., and his daughter Sebek-neferu. To this monarch must be attributed the making of the Fayûm province, and the conversion of the natural basin of the oasis into the celebrated Lake Moeris. At Semneh and Kummeh are recorded a series of high Nile registers taken during this reign.

Åmen-em-hāt IV., *Maāt-kheru-Rā*, cir. 2578-2569 B.C., seventh king of Dynasty XII. Very little is known

of this king, but his reign marks the decline of the XIIth Dynasty.

Åmen-hetep I., *Zezer-ka-Rā*, circ. B.C. 1562-1541,

Dynasty XVIII. Very little is known of the history

of this king, and for it we are chiefly dependent upon the inscriptions from the tombs of Áāḥmes and Pennekheb at El Kab. From them we learn that the king made a short but effectual raid into Cush or Nubia, and after that undertook a successful campaign against the Amukehak, who were probably a Libyan people. Ámen-ḥetep I. had two queens—Áāḥ-ḥetep II. and Sensenb—by whom he had six children. He was succeeded by Thothmes I., the son of the latter. The mummy of this king is in the Cairo Museum.

Ámen-ḥetep II., *Áa-kheperu-Rā*, Dynasty XVIII.,

cir. B.C. 1449-1423. His queen was Ta-āa, and he had several sons, by one of whom, Thothmes IV., he was succeeded. As usual, he made a raid into Asia, the success of which is chronicled upon the walls of the temples of Amada and Karnak. He appears also to have been into Nubia, as we hear of "the other enemy" being "hung upon the wall of the town of Napata to show forth all the victories of the king among all the people of the negro land."

Ámen-ḥetep III., *Neb-maāt-Rā*, the Nimmuriya of

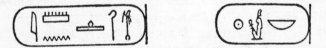

the Tel el Amarna tablets, Dynasty XVIII., cir. B.C. 1414-1379. His queens were Tyi, daughter of Yuaa and Thuaa, and Kirgipa. He had two sons and five daughters. His son Ámen-ḥetep IV. succeeded him. In the fifth year of his reign he went on a campaign into Ethiopia, but apart from this there is nothing to record. Under him began the first signs of that religious change which, in his son's time, became a reformation.

Ȧmen-ḥetep IV., *Nefer-kheperu-Rā*, Dynasty XVIII.

Called afterwards *Akh-cn-Ȧten*,

cir. B.C. 1383-1365. He married Nefertiti and had six
daughters. The fame of this king rests entirely upon
the reformation in the religion of the country, which
he brought about. He endeavoured to bring in a more
spiritual worship in the adoration of the Ȧten, or sun's
disk, and finding the opposition of the Theban priests to
be insurmountable, he removed his capital to a site now
known as Tel el Amarna, where, aided by his queen, he
sought to inculcate these new tenets, and to raise the
moral tone of the people. Of the old deities, Maāt, the
impersonation of truth, alone appears to have been
recognized. Unfortunately for the movement the king
died young, and within a few
years of his death all traces of
the Ȧten worship had passed
away. A successful endeavour,
though only temporary, was also
made to free art from the
priestly conventionalities which
were ruining it, and the arts and
crafts of this reign show distinct
efforts to copy from nature.
The sculptures and paintings of
birds, animals and plants are remarkable for their freedom from
the usual stilted representations.
(*See* ȦTEN.)

Ȧmen-Rā. A combination of
the gods Ȧmen and Rā. The
chief seat of his worship was at
Thebes. He is generally repre-

Ȧmen-Rā.

sented as standing, and holding in one hand the *user* sceptre, and in the other the *ānkh*. On his head are two tall plumes of feathers, from the back of which hangs a cord. (*See* Àmsu and Rā.)

Àment. A goddess who occasionally takes the place of Mut at Thebes. She was a feminine form of Àmen, sometimes represented with a sheep's head, and sometimes with a human head and the crown of Lower Egypt.

Àmenti. "The Hidden Land," the other world, which was in the west with the settting sun. Osiris is its lord, and he rules over the dead. An idea of the Egyptian conception of the Àmenti may be gathered from the pictures on the walls of the tombs of Seti I. and other kings, where the "Book of that which is in the Underworld," is inscribed and fully illustrated. The difficulties that have to be overcome by the Sun-god (Rā) during his nightly journey through the underworld are there described. It is divided into twelve sections, defined by fields, or cities, or dwellings, through all of which runs a river, on which, in a bark, the Sun travels again to the eastern horizon. Many demons of human and animal form, especially those in the form of serpents, beset his path. "He who dwells in Àmenti" is Osiris in the form of a mummy. The dead, being identified with Osiris, overcame all their adversaries, and as the Sun-god passed through the night to rise again in the east, so they expected in like manner to pass through Hades to the blessed life. An inscription of the time of Cleopatra speaks thus: "For as for Àmenti it is a land of sleep and darkness, a dwelling wherein those who are there remain. They sleep in their mummy forms, they nevermore awake to see their fellows, they behold neither their fathers nor their mothers, their heart is careless of their wives and children. . . . Since I came into this valley I know not where I am. I long for the water that floweth by me. I desire the breeze on the bank of the river, that

it may refresh my heart in its distress.   For the name
of the god who ruleth here is 'Utter Death,'" etc.

Amset or MESTHÁ, one of the four funerary genii to
whom the canopic jars were dedicated,
and who represented the cardinal
points.   Some texts say they were the
children of Horus, others that Osiris
was their father.   Figures of these
gods have been found in faïence, and
occasionally in bronze.   (*See* CANOPIC
JARS.)

Amsu, called also Min, Ámsi, Ármes,
or Khem, the ithyphallic nome god of
Panopolis, the *Ápu* of ancient Egypt,
and the modern Akhmîm (*q.v.*).
As representing the generative power
of nature he is sometimes identified
with Ámen-Rā and called Min-Ámen
or Ámen-Ámsu.   He is represented on
the monuments as a tightly swathed

Ámsu.

figure with only one arm free, that being raised
as if waving the *flagellum* it holds above the head.
For head-dress he wears the long plumes of Ámen.
Behind him there are usually growing plants.
Petrie found statues of this god at Coptos, and thinks
it probable that he was brought by his worshippers
from the land of Punt.

Ámt or PA-UÁZ.   The capital of *Ám-Pehu*, the
nineteenth nome of Lower Egypt.   The mound of Tell
Nebêsheh marks its site.   Uazit, Ámsu and Horus
formed the triad worshipped there.   It was celebrated
for its wine.

Amulets, or objects to which were attributed magical
powers of protection, were worn by the living and
disposed in and about the body of the deceased.   Some
are inscribed with *hekau*, i.e. "words of power,"

and several are mentioned in the "Book of the Dead." They were used from the earliest times. Every kind of stone or rock besides *frit* was used in their composition, but some were of more value, made in one particular stone or colour. Amethyst, garnet, turquoise, agate, jasper, lapis lazuli, felspar, obsidian, amber, hematite, malachite, granite, serpentine, and porphyry were all used, and the harder the substance the finer the work.

Scarab.   (*q.v.*)

Ānkh symbolizes life, possibly "the life which remains to one even after death," but it is difficult to tell what the figure represents. It was one of the most important of the amulets, and has been found in large numbers in every kind of material. It is sometimes depicted in combination with the *dād*, and has an independent existence ascribed to it.

Thet. The girdle buckle of Isis. An amulet usually made in some red material, such as carnelian, jasper, porphyry or glass. The colour was typical of the blood of Isis, which washed away the sins of the wearer. It was placed on the neck of the mummy, and frequently inscribed with chapter 156 of the "Book of the Dead."

Dād. An amulet placed on the neck of the mummy for its protection. The word signifies "firmness, stability, preservation." The 155th chapter of the "Book of the Dead" orders it to be made of gold. Like the *thet*, it had to be dipped in water in which *ānkham* flowers had lain.

Mut. An amulet usually made of gold, and which the rubric in the 157th chapter of the 'Book of the Dead" commands to be placed on the neck of the mummy on the day of burial. It symbolized the protection of Isis, the "mother" goddess.

Usekh. The collar of gold which was to be placed on the neck of the mummy on the day of burial, to give him power to free himself from his bandages. (*See* Rubric of 158th chapter of "Book of the Dead.")

Urs. An amulet representing the pillows, or head-rests, placed beneath the heads of the mummies. It is generally made of hematite. It is described in the earliest ritual of the "Book of the Dead," chapter 166.

Ab. An amulet representing the heart, the fountain of life, sometimes typifying the conscience.

Uzat. The Symbolic Eye, an amulet fastened to the wrist or arm, which protected the wearer from the evil eye, against the bites of serpents, and against words spoken in anger or malice.

The two were the Eyes of Horus, but in some instances the left represents the moon, the right the sun. (*See* EYE, THE SACRED.)

Nefer. An amulet signifying "good luck." It probably represents a musical instrument.

Sam. An amulet signifying union.

Akh or *Khu.* An amulet representing the sun's disk rising from the horizon. Found in the abdomen.

Shen. An amulet thought to represent the circle of the sun's orbit, and hence its object was to secure life to the deceased, enduring as the sun.

Uaz. An amulet representing a lotus column. It is invariably made of some green substance, and is symbolical of the gift of eternal youth.

Hez. The white crown of Upper Egypt.

Tesher. The red crown of Lower Egypt.

Menat. A sign of divine protection, the sight of which was supposed to drive away care. Most frequent in Saïte times.

Neh, symbolized protection, and was laid on the breast.

The Frog is not found in use until Dynasty XVIII. It was probably symbolical of the resurrection. The hieroglyphic sign means "myriads."

The Fingers. Generally found inside the abdomen of mummies.

The Stairs probably signify the throne of Osiris and the idea of raising up to heaven.

User. The royal sceptre, which gave dominion over heaven and earth.

The Plummet. To secure justice and moderation for the deceased.

Anastasi. *See* PAPYRI.

Ancestors. The names of ancestors of three and four generations are often inscribed with the names of the owner of a tomb. Frequently, however, they are only those of the maternal side of the house, the descent through the mother's side being reckoned of more importance than that through the father. Although much attention was paid by relatives to the tombs of their fathers, and festivals were held in honour of the dead, this never amounted to actual ancestor worship.

The "HALL OF ANCESTORS" is a small chamber taken from Karnak to the Bibliothèque Nationale in Paris by M. Prisse. It is so called because it contains a representation of Thothmes III. making offerings to sixty-one of his predecessors. Similar scenes occur at Sakkâra and Abydos.

Ȧnḥur, Ȧnḥour or **Ȧnḥer.** A form of the Sun god worshipped at Thinis and Sebennytus. As "slayer of the enemies" he is seen standing in the prow of the sun bark in a warlike attitude, with a lance in his hand. He was in later times united with Shu to form the dual god, Ȧnḥur-Shu. Like the other solar gods, he came to be associated with a lioness-headed goddess called Meḥit. His mother was the Sebennytic form of Hathor, called Ḥer-t. His head-dress is four plumes.

Ānit. A form of the goddess Hathor, wife of the Theban god Mentu. A text at Dendera speaks of her as mother of Horus.

Ȧnḥur.

Ānkh. *See* AMULETS.

Ȧnnu, five miles north of Cairo, was the centre of the worship of Rā. There was another town of the same name, called "Annu of the South," near Thebes. (*See* HELIOPOLIS.)

Ȧntef. A name common in the XIth and XIIth Dynasties, and family name of some kings of the XIth Dynasty. Little is known of these kings; but from the humbleness of their tombs (simple pyramids of brickwork) it has been supposed that they were only local chieftains reigning in the Thebaïd. Of **Ȧntef I.**, cir. B.C. 2985, the coffin

Ānit.

and mummy were found by Arabs at the foot of the
western mountain of the Theban Necropolis. The
coffin of **Ȧntef II.**, cir. B.C. 2945, surnamed *"Āa"*
(i.e. the Great), was found by Brugsch Bey in 1854.

It is now in the Louvre.   Another **Ȧntef (III.)**,
cir. B.C. 2940, bore the second name, *Rā-seshes-up-
maāt*. His gilded coffin is in the British Museum.

Ȧntef IV., *Hor-uaḥ-ānkh*, cir. B.C. 2902, is only

known by his brick pyramid at Thebes and the
mention of his name in the Abbot Papyrus. A stela
showing the king with his four favourite dogs was in
the pyramid.

Ȧntef V., *Nub-kheperu-Rā*, cir. B.C. 2852. An in-

scription containing the decree for the degradation by
this king of " Tetà, son of Min-ḥetep " probably one of
the feudal princes or a very high official, for " har-
bouring enemies," is in the Gizeh Museum.

Ȧntef VI., *S-ānkh-ka-Rā*, cir. B.C. 2786. Ninth

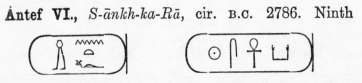

and last king of Dynasty XI. An expedition to the
land of Punt was undertaken in his reign.

Antha.

Antha. A goddess imported from Asia, probably of Phoenician origin, often mentioned in the inscriptions of Ramses II. and Ramses III. She is a kind of war goddess and is represented armed with helmet, shield, and lance, and swinging a battle-axe. She is called "Lady of heaven and queen of the gods," and is usually seen in the company of Reshpu (*q.v.*).

Anubis or Anpu. The god who presided over embalming, and especially a god of the dead. His cult was very general throughout Egypt, but it seems to have had its centre at Lycopolis (Asyût). There was also a Lycopolis in the Delta where he was worshipped, and this fact may have given rise to the apparent doubling of the god, for the texts speak of Anubis of the north and Anubis of the south. He is said to be the son of Osiris and Nephthys, and to have swallowed his father Osiris. As a nature god—his father being the sun—he may represent the twilight. He is depicted with a human body and the head of a jackal. One of his names is "Ap-uat" (*q.v.*).

Anpu.

Anukit. A goddess, wife of KHNEMU and third in the triad of Elephantiné. Her distinguishing

Anukit,

head-dress is a crown of feathers, though sometimes she wears only the crown of Upper Egypt. She is called "Lady of Sati," Sati being the name for the island of Sehêl, where there was a temple to the goddesses Sati and Ānukit. She is possibly of Nubian origin.

Ȧnupt. A goddess found at Dendera. She represents the feminine principle of Ȧnpu (*q.v.*).

Apēum, the,—often but erroneously called the Serapēum—was the palace in which the sacred bulls were lodged at Memphis.

Apis Mausoleum, the. The excavated vaults at Sakkâra, in which the sacred Apis bulls were buried after being embalmed. These are often erroneously called the Serapēum. (*See* SERAPĒUM.)

Ȧpepi (Greek Apophis). The great serpent, the impersonation of spiritual evil ; and head of the powers of darkness against whom the sun under the form of Rā or Horus waged his daily war. He is represented as a serpent of many folds having a knife stuck into each. As the sun went towards the west, he was confronted by Ȧpepi with his troops of fiends called Qettu, Sebau, Sheta, &c., and battled with them all night until dawn. The 39th chapter of the "Book of the Dead" is devoted to details of the combat. There is also a work entitled "The Book of the Overthrowing of Ȧpepi" (see below ; also NESI-ȦMSU), which treats entirely of this opponent of Rā who is, through Rā, the opponent of all souls of deceased persons. The dead were identified with Osiris, who was another form of the sun-god, lord of the underworld ; therefore on the sun's ultimate victory depended their safety. In some instances we find Ȧpepi identified with Typhon, and in Graeco-Roman times with Set. "Ȧpepi was never called a god. He therefore represents, not a regularly occurring phenomenon, but an irregular and occasional one. He is the strong, dark, storm-cloud, and is overcome by the fire and flinty sword of the Sun-god and forced back into his subterranean cavern. One of his names is the Roarer; he is represented as blind, and another of his names, Ubar, signifies 'the blind one,' like the Latin Cacus, or Caeculus." (Renouf.)

Apepi I. and II. (Apophis).

Two of the Hyksos kings. Should be placed probably in Dynasty XV. It is thought by many Egyptologists that Joseph served under the latter.

Apepi, Book of the Overthrowing of A work which forms about a third of the funeral papyrus of Nesi-Amsu (*q.v.*). It treats of the daily battle between Rā and Apepi (*q.v.*), recalling certain chapters of the "Book of the Dead," notably chapters 7, 31, 33, and 35 to 39, from which the author has evidently borrowed. The title tells us that the book was recited in the temple of Amen-Rā in the Apts every day. It contains fifteen chapters, in some of which there is a monotonous repetition of phrases. They treat of the various methods for destroying the fiend, and are both mythical and magical. The name of Apepi was to be written in green on a papyrus and burnt; wax figures were also to be made of several fiends, and, after being defiled, were to be burnt. The most interesting part of the work is that which gives an account of the creation, and of how men and women were formed by the tears shed by the god Kheperà. It is called "The Book of Knowing the Evolutions of Rā."

That the work is of some antiquity is shown by the variant readings which occur, but no other copy is yet known. It differs from other funeral papyri in speaking of the deceased as *P-āa* (the Pharaoh) instead of as the Osiris.

Åpes. A tortoise-headed deity (?), substituted in some texts for the serpent Åpepi (*q.v.*).

Apes or **Apet**. Another name for TA-URT (*q.v.*).

Apis. The name of the sacred bull which was worshipped by the Egyptians from the earliest times.

Apis.

The cult was said to have been introduced by Mena (Ist Dynasty), the most ancient discoveries of his worship being at Memphis, though another story says that it was introduced into Memphis from Heliopolis in the IInd Dynasty. But it was not until later times that the Apis bull became of so much importance. Renouf says: "The triumph of the symbol over the thought is most sensibly visible in the development of the worship of the Apis bull." The Apis symbolized "the second life of Ptah," the god of Memphis. He was born of a cow, to whom a deity had descended in the form of lightning or a ray of moonlight. According to Herodotus he was black, with a square white spot on the forehead; on his back was the figure of an eagle, in the tail double hairs, and on the tongue a beetle. The priests searched for such an animal throughout Egypt, and when found he was brought first to Nicopolis, in Lower Egypt, and then with great pomp and ceremony to Memphis. When he died, the body was embalmed and put in an enormous sarcophagus. The so-called *Serapēum* at Sakkâra is a great Apis mausoleum, where numbers of these sacred bulls were buried. The stelae that covered a large part of the walls of this vast tomb were of immense importance historically, as giving the dates of birth and burial of the bulls, that is to say the exact year in a king's reign. Apis was represented with a disk and uraeus between the horns. It was supposed that, at his death—like a human being—he became one with Osiris.

Apis. Greek name for *Nut-ent-Hāpi*, the capital of the third nome of Lower Egypt, the modern Kom el Hism. Chief deity, Hathor.

Aphroditopolis. The Greek name for *Tep-àḥet*, capital of the twenty-second nome of Upper Egypt, the modern Atfih. Chief deity, Hathor.

Aphroditopolis. The Greek name for *Tebt*, capital of the tenth nome of Upper Egypt, the modern Itfu. Chief deity, Hathor.

Apollinopolis Magna. The Greek name for *Tebt*, the capital of the second nome of Upper Egypt, the modern Edfu. Chief deity, Ḥor-beḥutet (*q.v.*).

Àpt. That part of Thebes which lay on the east bank of the Nile. It was divided into "Northern Àpt," represented by Karnak, and "Southern Àpt," the modern Luxor.

Àp-uat—literally "the opener of the ways." He is one of the forms of Anubis, and was worshipped at Asyût. His office was to introduce the souls of the departed into the "divine hidden land." (*See* ANUBIS.)

Ārār. Name of the Uraeus, the serpent which was worn on the forehead of gods and kings. It was an emblem of divinity and royalty. (*See* URAEUS.)

Ārār.

Arch. Although the Egyptians were acquainted with the arch they but rarely used it. The earliest specimen of a true arch is found in a IVth Dynasty mastăba at Medûm.

Architects. Since architecture was Egypt's principal art, all others being more or less accessory or subsidiary, it is natural that of all artists the architects should have been most honoured. The names of many are recorded on stelae in museums· and in tombs. The office sometimes appears to have been hereditary, and sometimes even a royal prince did not disdain to take the office of " chief of all the constructions of Upper and Lower Egypt," the holder of which was apparently highly honoured by the king. At times it was combined with the priestly office, as in the case of Bak-en-Khensu, first prophet of Åmen, and principal architect at Thebes under Seti I. and Ramses II., whose sepulchral statue is preserved at Munich. The most famous architect whose name has come down to us is Sen-mut, the favourite of Hatshepsut, and builder of Dêr-el-Baḥri.

Åri-hes-nefer.

Åri-hes-nefer. This Ethiopian god is a son of Rā and Bast, and was one of the chief deities of the tenth nome of Upper Egypt. There are the remains of a temple to his honour on the Island of Philae. He is represented with a lion's head and the double crown, or with a human head and a headdress consisting of the disk, ram's horns, plumes and two uraei:

Årit. One of the gates of Hades, guarded by a mummiform creature called Āau.

Arms. (*See* WEAPONS.)

Arrows. Wood and reed arrows from twenty-two to thirty-four inches long, tipped with hard wood, flint, or metal have been found. Those with hard wood and flint heads were probably only used by huntsmen. As a weapon of war the arrow was tipped with a bronze head, which was sometimes barbed, and sometimes triangular and made with three or four blades. The shaft of the weapon was winged with three feathers like a modern arrow.

Arsinoë. A town in the Fayûm dedicated to Arsinoë, the sister-wife of Ptolemy Philadelphus. The ancient site is now represented by the modern town of Medinet el Fayûm.

Asher. That part of Thebes lying to the south of the temple of Amen at Karnak and dedicated to Mut, the wife of Amen, to whom Amen-hetep III. dedicated a temple. Later on Shishak placed there many lioness-headed statues of the goddess.

Assà, *Dād-ka-Rā*, IVth Dynasty, cir. B.C. 3580.

Traces of this king have been found in the Wady Hammamât and the Wady Maghârah. The Proverbs of Ptah-hetep (Prisse Papyrus) date back to this reign.

Astarte. A goddess imported from Syria, probably at the time of the great Kheta war under Ramses II., but not popular until later. Her title is "lady of horses and chariots." The eastern quarter of Tanis was dedicated to her. Sometimes she is represented with the head of a lioness.

Astronomy. Great attention was paid to this science, and though, judging from our modern knowledge of the subject, the Egyptians only knew the rudiments, from the standpoint of Diodorus Siculus, they were very learned. "There is no country where the positions and movements of the stars are observed with such accuracy as in Egypt. They have kept, during an incredible number of years, registers where these observations are recorded." But, unfortunately, none of these "registers" have come down to us.

Thoth was the god who taught men the science of the heavens. An important part of the priestly college was the school of astronomy. The priests of Rā seem to have been the first to recognize the importance of this study, and their keenness of sight is indicated in some of the titles they bear, as "great of sight," "the reader who knows the face of the heavens, the great of sight in the mansion of the Prince of Hermonthis." The astronomers attached to the temples were called "watchers of the night." They knew at least five of our planets, and some of the constellations have been identified. Jupiter, Saturn, Mercury, Mars and Venus were depicted under various forms, but were not actually worshipped. Orion (Sahu) and Sirius (Sothis), according to our interpretation, were supposed to be the abodes respectively of the souls of Horus and Isis. They are represented in various places as human beings standing in the little barks in which they sailed the ocean of the sky, or, as at Dendera, Orion as a man beckoning to Sirius as a cow reclining in the bark behind him.

"The constellations were reckoned to be thirty-six in number, the thirty-six *decani* to whom were attributed mysterious powers, and of whom the star Sothis was queen—Sothis transformed into the star of Isis, when Orion (Sahu) became the star of Osiris." (Maspero.)

The chief maps of the sky preserved on temple and tomb walls are those at the Ramessēum, Dendera, and in the tomb of Seti I. at Thebes. Star tables are found in the tombs of Ramses IV. and Ramses IX. at Thebes, but they are carelessly done, as probably they were only considered as part of the decoration of the tomb. The constellations were represented as stars outlining the bodies of animals. Our constellation, the "Plough," was their "Haunch." Behind the *haunch* came a female hippopotamus, and on her back a crocodile. A couchant lion faced the *haunch*, with a curious composite animal underneath.

Atef. *See* CROWNS.

Åten. The name given to the solar disk, the worship of which under that name was the chief cult under Åmen-ḥetep IV. (Akh-en-Åten), who tried to make it the religion of the country. Until this period the Åten had rarely stood alone, although the phrase " Rā in his Åten " is not uncommon. The god is always represented as the solar disk with rays extending from it, each terminating in a hand, and never in human form. The hands usually hold the $\stackrel{\circ}{\mathrm{T}}$, which they present to the king and queen. The centre of his cult was at the modern Tel el Amarna, and in the hills behind are the tombs of his worshippers. In one tomb is preserved a very fine hymn to the Åten (published by Bouriant in " Mémoires de la Mission au Caire "). (See KHU-EN-ÅTEN and Hymns.)

Åten.

Athribis. Greek name for *Het-ta herabt*, the capital of the tenth nome of Lower Egypt, the modern Benha el Asal. The chief deity was Heru-Khent-khati.

Avaris. The Greek name of *Ḥat-uārt*, a city mentioned by Josephus (*contra Apion*) as having been built by the Hyksos, and eventually their last stronghold in Egypt, it being the last place to give way before the

new Egyptian dynasty, which drove out the invaders.
Its site is doubtful, some identifying it with Tanis;
possibly it was on the coast near Pelusium.

B

Ba. In Egyptian pneumatology the Ba was the
anima, the soul of man, which at the death of the body
flew to the gods.   But it did not remain there entirely,
for it came back at intervals to comfort the mummy.

The Ba.

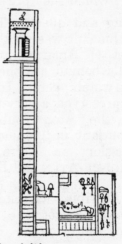

Ba visiting mummy.

It was represented in the form of a bird with human
head, and hands which frequently hold the *ānkh* (*q.v.*)
and the *nif* (*q.v.*)   Thus in one scene it is represented
as flying down the tomb shaft to the deceased.   In
another it is resting with out-spread wings on the top

of the mummy. In this form it is sometimes sculptured on a sarcophagus lid. The conception was not, perhaps, wholly immaterial, for a chapter in the "Book of the Dead" assures abundance of food to the Ba of the deceased.

Baal. *See* BAL.

Bahr Yûsuf. The great canal which runs parallel with the Nile on the west side, commencing in the Crocodilopolite Nome nearly opposite Akhmîm, and joining the Nile at the modern El Wasta in the Arsinoïte Nome, a distance by river of 350 miles. It is rather a continuous series of canals than one, and it is only navigable throughout its length during the inundation. "It is evident from Strabo and Ptolemy that, in their time, the important canal known as the Bahr Yûsuf did not flow as it does now. If, as is probably the case, its bed is natural, and not the work of man, a great part of it would have been silted up in the time of the Greek writers, and according to an Arab tradition it was reopened by the famous Sultan Saladin, who then gave it his name of Yûsuf." We are thus led to the conclusion that, according to the Greek writers, the Bahr Yûsuf in its present course cannot be very old. It is probably a work of nature enlarged and modified by the hand of man. Possibly the kings of the XIIth Dynasty may have begun this system of water regulation in connection with the works of Lake Moeris, which is always attributed to them." After Derût the Bahr Yûsuf changes its name successively to Ibrahimîyeh, Sohagîyeh, and Raiân. Its ancient name is unknown.

Bak-en-ren-f. *See* BOCCHORIS.

Bal. A form of Baal, worshipped in the eastern part of the Delta, with a temple at Tanis. He was introduced from Phoenicia after the wars of the XIXth Dynasty. He is a form of the war god.

Ball. *See* Toys.

Bakh, the Greek Bacis, was the name of the sacred bull at *Hermonthis* (Erment) in which the god Mentu was incarnate. (*See* Mentu.)

Ba-neb-tattu. The god of Mendes. He is represented with a ram's head, a fact which gave rise, by a curious error, to the statement of the classic authors that the Egyptians called the goat Mendes. His title is "living soul of Rā."

Ba-n-neter. Third king of Dynasty II., reigned forty-seven(?) years. In his reign the female succession to the throne was secured.

Barks, Sacred. The heavens being conceived of as an ocean, the solar gods were often spoken of as progressing in their barks. The sun's two barks are the best known of these. At his birth in the morning he entered the *Sektit* bark,* ⸾⳨⸗ which took him to his most southern point at noon. He then travelled till sunset in the *Mazit* or *Madet* bark ⸗⳧. During the night he changed into different barks, until received again into the *Sektit* bark next morning. The pictures of these barks vary. Sometimes the boat is extremely simple and contains only the sun disk. At others it is large, with a cabin or shrine in the centre for the chief gods, who are accompanied by other gods before and behind. Sometimes there are rowers, at others it is self-propelled either with or without a helmsman to guide it. Tum and Kheperá are the gods who most frequently accompany Rā. The bark of Ptah-Seker-Osiris was called *Hennu* and that of Nun *Neshmet*. The temples had models of these boats, in which in some cases the symbol of the god was kept. These barks were carried in procession round the temple at stated times. (*See* Moon.)

* Erman reverses this order, and calls the *Mazit* the bark of the morning, and the *Sektit* the bark of the sunset.

Basalt. This volcanic rock was highly valued for the making of statues. It was difficult to obtain, not being found in the Nile valley, but in the desert. It was too precious a material to be used for mere architectural purposes. It is also extremely hard to work, yet the finish on statues and sarcophagi sculptured from this stone is as perfect as could be produced in these days. The finest specimens belong to the XXVIth Dynasty.

Bast. A solar goddess who represented the gentle and useful heat of the sun, as opposed to Sekhet, the fierce heat. She is represented cat-headed, holding in one hand a sistrum, in the other,—over the arm of which she carries a basket,— a shield. The cat was sacred to her. The chief seat of her worship was at Bubastis — the modern Tell Basta — where a great temple was built to her. Her husband was Her-hekennu, a form of Horus.

Bast.

Bastinado. This form of punishment was used for men, women, and children. Wall paintings show the victim held by his arms and legs to the ground by two men.

Beards. For purposes of cleanliness the Egyptian gentleman went clean shaven in everyday life, but on great occasions it was customary to wear an artificial beard. This was made of hair very tightly plaited and fastened by straps on to the head-dress or behind the ears. The king wore a longer beard than his subjects. Figures of the gods are usually represented with a pointed beard curled up at the end—and on the coffins of the mummies the same form is frequently found, the deceased having become an Osirian, i.e. made one with Osiris. Only foreign slaves and shepherds were allowed to wear beards. Prisoners were not allowed to shave.

Beer. The "barley wine" of the ancient Egyptians. There were four sorts in use under the old Empire; in later times that from Qede, in Asia Minor, was esteemed the most highly, and during the Ptolemaic period the Zythos beer was the favourite. It was made from the "corn of Upper Egypt," i.e. barley; but how prepared is unknown. One papyrus mentions a beer tax at Memphis which amounted to 45 talents 3100 drachmae in one month.

Bennu. The name of a sacred bird, an emblem of the resurrection, and consecrated to Osiris. It seems

to have been the forerunner of the Greek Phoenix. It is represented as a heron-like bird with two long feathers flowing from the back of its head. Its name signifies "that which revolves," or "turns back." The legend at Heliopolis was that the bird rose singing from the flames which came out of a certain tree, its song being so beautiful that even Rā himself listened. In old texts the soul of the deceased was compared to the Bennu bird.

Bennu bird.

Bes. A god whose worship dates from remote times, but who was of foreign origin, having been introduced from the land of Punt. He is a god of somewhat complex character. In the "Book of the Dead" he is identified with Set, and in this aspect would seem to be of an evil nature. He also invariably figures in birth scenes in all the *mammisi* of Egyptian temples, where his function could not have been evil. In another form he appears to be a kind of Bacchus, for he presides over

Bes.

dancing and music and gaiety. As such he is represented frequently with an instrument—a harp, or
cymbals. He is also a war god, being often depicted
armed, with sword-hand uplifted. In aspect he is
grotesque and hideous. He is a crooked, fat dwarf,
wearing a beast's skin with the tail hanging down
behind. He is bearded, and frequently his tongue is
extended. His distinguishing head-dress is a crown of
feathers, somewhat like that of Ānukit. At various
times he was identified with different gods—with Horus
when he wears the side-lock of youth, with Sopt and
with Harpocrates. Unlike most of the Egyptian gods,
he is represented invariably front face. His figure has
been found on Babylonian, Persian, and Gnostic seals.
It frequently decorates Egyptian articles of toilet.

Birth-house. *See* MAMMISI.

Boats. One of the most important trades of ancient
Egypt was boat building. The river was their great
highway of travel. Boats were, roughly speaking, of
three kinds; light skiffs, that could be easily carried
from one point to another, and larger vessels for
freight, and a grander kind corresponding to the
modern dahabîya, or house-boat. The former were
made of reeds bound tightly together and smeared
inside with pitch. Such a boat was Moses' "ark of
bulrushes." These, as a rule, were only large enough
to contain one or two people. They were punted with
a pole, or propelled by a paddle. A papyrus boat was
supposed to be a protection against crocodiles. The
larger boats were built of wood—probably acacia—the
masts were of fir imported from Syria, the sails were
occasionally made of papyrus fibre, but probably also
of linen (*see* Ez. xxvii. 7). When the boat was that
of a god or of a grandee, these were elaborately ornamented with painting or embroidery. Boats of this
kind had spacious cabins gaily decorated. Some of
them measured over 100 ft. in length, taking twenty-
two rowers a side when coming down stream. The

steering gear was of the most primitive kind, consisting
merely of one or two enormous oars or paddles.   The
only sails represented are square.   There are many
pictures of boats on the tomb and temple walls.   (*See*
BARKS.)

Bocchoris. The Greek name given by Manetho to
Bak-en-ren-f, a Saïte king of the XXIVth Dynasty,
who, it appears, was scarcely independent of the
Ethiopian kings.

Book of the Dead. The name given to *Pert em hru*,
which may be translated, " coming forth by day," or
" manifested in the light."   It has also been called the
" Funeral Ritual," and more fancifully and ignorantly,
the Egyptian Bible.   It has been found in many
papyri, and chapters from it are inscribed on the walls
of tombs and pyramids, and on sarcophagi and mummy
wrappings.   No one copy contains all the chapters
(about 200), and in no case is the same sequence
observed all through.   The chapters " are as independent of one another as the Hebrew Psalms," and like
them, were composed at different times.   The longest
known copy is in a Turin papyrus, which contains 165
chapters.   The difficulties of translating the work are
immense, for even in the early times the text had
become corrupt, and the constant copying of it by the
uninitiated had rendered it most obscure.   This is
increased by the fact that the work is mythological
throughout, and assumes the knowledge of all current
myths on the part of the reader.   The lofty ideas set
forth in some chapters seem to stand out in great
contrast with the apparently gross conceptions found
in others ; but in the latter case some esoteric meaning may be imagined, of which the key is lost.
" The Beatification of the Dead is the main subject
of every chapter."   The deceased was supposed to
recite the chapters in order that he might gain power
and enjoy the privileges of his new life.   His desire
was to have all the powers he had lost at death

restored to him. Of punishment almost nothing is said. The highest bliss was to be identified with the gods, and to have the power of transforming himself into anything he pleased.

Among the principal gods mentioned are Rā, Seb, Nut, Osiris, Isis, Horus, Set, Nephthys, Ptah, Thoth, Khnemu, and Tum. The Theban gods are conspicuous by their absence.

The oldest papyrus copy of the work is of the XVIIIth Dynasty. The earlier copies are not so copiously illustrated as later ones, the vignettes gradually becoming of more and more importance. They are in many cases brilliantly coloured. Most of the versions agree in saying that the oldest chapter is the sixty-fourth, the Turin papyrus adding that it was discovered by a son of Khufu, of the IVth Dynasty; another text ascribes it to the Ist Dynasty. It is called "The chapter of coming forth by day in the underworld." Other chapters are called, " of coming forth by day and living after death "; "of driving away shame from the heart of the deceased"; "a hymn of praise to Rā when he setteth in the land of life;" "of bringing words of magical power to the deceased in the underworld "; " of not dying a second time "; "of giving air in the underworld"; "of changing into whatsoever form he pleaseth "; " of making the soul to be united to its body "; " of knowing the souls of the west "; "of making a man go into heaven to the side of Rā." There are directions that certain chapters shall be written on certain amulets. The most valuable English translations are those by Sir P. le P. Renouf, in the Proceedings of the Society of Biblical Archaeology, vols. xiv., xv. xvi., &c., and by E. W. Budge.

Bow. It was made of a round piece of wood, from 5 to 5½ ft. in length, either almost straight, or curved in at the centre. A groove or notch at each end received the string, or else it was fixed to a projecting piece of horn. The bow-string was of hide, catgut, or string. On the monuments the archers are represented drawing the bow in two different ways, either to the breast, or in the much more effective way, when the bow is held so high that the arrow-line is level with the eye. (*See* ARROWS.)

Bricks. Ordinary oblong bricks were made simply of clay mixed with chopped straw and a little sand, materials easily obtained, and suitable to the climate, quickly drying by exposure to the sun. Tomb paintings shew us brick-makers kneading the paste with the feet, pressing it into hard wooden moulds, and laying the blocks out in rows to dry. After an exposure of about half a day, these blocks were stacked in such a manner as to allow the air to circulate freely about them, and remained thus for a week or two. For the poorer dwellings the exposure was only for a few hours before the building was commenced. In size the bricks usually measured $8·7 \times 4·3 \times 5·5$; but a larger size was also used, measuring $15·0 \times 7·1 \times 5·5$. They were marked in various ways, those made in the royal brickfields being stamped with the cartouche of the reigning Pharaoh. A few glazed bricks have been found of the period of the Ramses, at Tell Defenneh and Nebesheh. Wooden brick-moulds have also been found. The labour of brick-making was imposed on captives, the Hebrews not being the only subject people thus made use of. A painting at Thebes, executed long before the Mosaic period, shows us Asiatic prisoners making bricks for a temple to Amen; and a passage in a papyrus (Anastasi III., iii.) confirms the supposition we are led to by Exodus v. 8, that a certain quantity of bricks was required daily from each worker.

Bridge. Up to the present time we only know of one bridge in Ancient Egypt and that appears to have crossed a canal at Zaru, a frontier town on the Delta. An illustration of it may be seen on the outside wall (north end) of the Hypostyle Hall at Karnak.

Bronze. The favourite metal of the Egyptians. Even after the invention or discovery of bronze, flint implements were used. The proportions of the copper and tin used by the Egyptians in making this metal vary according to the use for which it was destined. Vases, mirrors and weapons contain from 80 to 85 parts of copper and 15 to 20 of tin. Bronze was largely used for making statuettes and miniature figures, but these do not occur until after the XVIIIth Dynasty. The bronze intended for mirrors and fine work has often an alloy of gold or silver. No representation of the working of this metal is seen on tomb walls. (*See* COPPER AND TIN.)

Bubastis. The Greek name for *Pa-Bast* capital of the eighteenth nome of Lower Egypt, the modern Tell Basta. Chief deity, Bast, a goddess frequently represented with a cat's head.

Bull. Of all the sacred animals in Egypt perhaps the bull received the most attention. In the ithyphallic cult he is represented by Khem. Ámen is addressed as "bull, fair of face." The Theban kings took a title "strong bull," possibly from Bakut, the name under which the bull sacred to Mentu was worshipped in Erment. The bull was the emblem of strength and courage. (*See* APIS and MNEVIS and SERAPÉUM.)

Busiris. Greek name for *Pa-Áusàr*, capital of the ninth nome of Lower Egypt, the modern Abusîr. The chief deity was Osiris (*q.v.*).

Buto. The Greek name for *Pa-Uazt*, the capital of the nineteenth nome of Lower Egypt; the modern Nebesheh. Chief deity Uazit (*q.v.*).

Buto. Goddess of the North. *See* UAZIT.

C

Calendar. *See* YEAR.

Cambyses. *See* PERSIAN DYNASTY.

Canopic Jars. The four jars in which were placed the embalmed viscera of the deceased. The name is said to have been adopted, because of the resemblance the jars bore to a form of Canopus worshipped in the place of that name. The cover of each jar was in the form of a head, the heads being those of the four genii —children either of Horus or Osiris according to different texts—who represented the cardinal points, and to whom the jars were dedicated. The jar covered

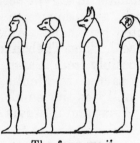

The four genii.

by the man-head of Mesṭhá or Ȧmseṭ, representing the south, contained the stomach and large intestines. That covered by the dog-head of Hāpi representing the north, contained the small intestines. The jackal head of Tuamāutef, who represented the east, covered the jar containing the lungs and heart, while the hawk-head of Qebḥsennuf, god of the west, covered the liver and gall bladder. These jars do not appear until the XVIIIth Dynasty, and after the XXVIth Dynasty they gradually fell into disuse. In the earlier period they were made of alabaster or some fine kind of stone ; later on of green and blue glazed faïence, also of wood, and still later of terra-cotta. Occasionally solid wooden jars are found. An inscription—incised on stone ones and painted on wooden ones—was usually placed on each, and from these inscriptions we learn that Mestha was under the protection of Isis, Hāpi under that of Nephthys, Tuamāutef was guarded by Neith, and Qebhsennuf by Selk. The four jars were very frequently placed in a sepulchral chest. Jars of the same shape, containing mummied bodies of various sacred animals, have been found at several places. (British Museum : 2nd Egyptian Gallery ; wall case.)

Cartouche. The name given to the elliptical enclosure with a line at the end, in which was inscribed the royal name. It may be the representation of an elongated seal. The " cartouche " of a Pharaoh is his name enclosed by this line. Only royal names were written thus. Each king had at least two cartouches, one containing his prenomen or divine name, the other his dynastic cognomen.

Caste. It was supposed, before the great advance in Egyptology that was brought about by the decipherment of the hieroglyphs, that caste existed in ancient Egypt. But more recent discoveries have com pletely done away with this idea. There were no impassable barriers between class and class, or between one profession and another.

Cat. This animal was sacred to Bast, who is frequently represented with the head of a cat. Its name

mau appears to be onomatopoetic. The cat often figures in vignettes in the "Book of the Dead," where it sometimes holds a knife, with which to slay a serpent. But the meaning here is obscure. That the animal was much venerated is shown by the fact of the numberless mummied cats that have been found, especially at Bubastis, Sakkâra, and Beni Hasan. It was perhaps a symbol of the Sun-god and day, slaying the serpent, the emblem of evil and darkness. On tomb walls we see the cat accompanying his master in his little skiff when he goes fowling in the marshes, and it has been suggested that the animal was taught to retrieve. Many figures of cats of different sizes have been found, in bronze and faïence.

Chief of the Chancellors and Royal Seal Bearer. A class of officials existing after the XIIth and before the XVIIIth Dynasty. They appear to have " acted for the king in matters connected with the treasury and taxes, and over the royal decrees and public documents bearing the king's seal." Light is perhaps thrown on the office and power of these officials in the story of the elevation of Joseph, by the Pharaoh, to be the royal seal bearer and head of the civil administration.

Cippi of Horus are small stelae or tablets, from 3 in. × 2 in. to 20 in. × 16 in. in size, having on them magical formulae, and constituting a form of talisman for initiates. They are of late date, probably later than the XXVIth Dynasty.

Circumcision. That this was a custom is asserted by Herodotus, and confirmed by pictures on the monuments. Very little, if any, significance was given to the practice from a religious point of view.

Cleopatra. The name of several wives and daughters of different Ptolemies. The first Cleopatra was a Syrian Princess, who married Ptolemy Epiphanes (V.). Cleopatra II. seems to have enjoyed a co-regency with her brother-husband Philometor. Indeed the six or seven queens of the name all seem to have had almost equal power with their husbands. The great Cleopatra was the VIth or VIIth, according to different historians. She has left evidence of her reign on the walls of the temple of Dendera, where her portrait may be seen, together with that of her son Caesarion.

Cobalt. It was supposed, until recently, that the Egyptians did not make use of cobalt in preparing their blue pigments. But experiments on some small objects of the later time of the New Empire proved the supposition to be wrong; a quantitative analysis yielding 2·86 per cent. of oxide of cobalt. A. W. Hofmann asserts that cobalt was added to the glassy fluxes in the form of a cobalt mineral, but finds it impossible to define this mineral. Cobalt has been found in a mineral called masrit, discovered by Johnson Pasha in a remote part of Egypt. Masrit contains 1·02 per cent. of oxide of cobalt.

Coffins. The style of the wooden coffins varies considerably throughout the dynasties. The earliest examples are rectangular, unpainted, with a short inscription cut on the lid, and also round the four sides. On the lid was a human face, made of pieces of wood pegged on. In the XIth and XIIth Dynasties the shape was still rectangular, with decorations in stripes of gaudy colours, or in the case of better ones, inscribed inside and outside with chapters from the "Book of the Dead" in hieratic. We also find coffins with human faces at this period. Isis and Nephthys are represented in some part of the decorations very often kneeling, and seeming to embrace the coffin with their wings.

Later, about the time of the XIXth Dynasty, the decorations became very elaborate. The coffin took the shape, more or less, of the mummy, with a well-modelled face, having the eyes let in in some harder material, and wooden hands crossed over the breast. The mummy was enclosed in two, three, and even four elaborately painted coffins. The texts record the titles of the deceased, also chapters from the "Book of the Dead." The scenes represent the deceased adoring the gods. These coffins were varnished with a thick yellow varnish. Coffins of XXIInd to XXVIth Dynasties have scenes of the weighing of the heart in the judgment hall of Osiris, and pictures of the Ba (*q.v.*) visiting the body. After this period the art degenerated. The lids were fastened on with wooden dowels, the places where these were inserted being plastered up and painted over.

Coinage. *See* MONEY.

Colossi. These were placed in front of the temples. There were two, four, or six representing the founder of the temple. So much was thought of these figures that if a Pharaoh would not be at the pains to have his own portrait executed he would erase the names of his predecessor from some existing statues and substitute his own. But few of these are left standing. The most celebrated were the statues of Ȧmen-ḥetep III. at Thebes, one of which was called the "Vocal Memnon" (*q.v.*). They, like most colossal statues, are seated figures. Their height is 52 ft. The colossus of Ramses II. at the Ramessēum at Thebes was the largest known, being 57½ ft. high. It lies shattered on the ground. A head similar to that of this statue was found near the south side of the Ramessēum, and was transported to England. It is now in the British Museum. At Memphis lies another statue of Ramses II., 31½ ft. high. The two seated colossi in front of the temple at Luxor are 45 ft. high. All these figures of Ramses are of granite. The colossal figures carved out of the gritstone hill at Abu Simbel, which form the façade of the temple of Ramses II., are about 66 ft. high without the pedestal. In a tomb now almost destroyed at El Bersheh there was a representation on the wall of the transportation of a colossus The chief colossi belong to the period of the New Empire, after which time the taste for them seems to have died out.

Combs. The earliest form of comb known dates from what is usually called the " Pre-historic " period, and is made of ivory, with rude but vigorous carvings of animals on the back. Specimens of this period are very rare. The later kind is of wood, with teeth on both sides exactly like our modern tooth comb, except that the teeth are sometimes wider on the one side than on the other. The flat surface along the centre is frequently ornamented with carving or inlay.

Commerce. *See* TRADE.

Cones. *See* FUNERARY CONES.

Copper. The copper used by the Egyptians in the making of their bronze came chiefly from the Wady Maghârah, in the peninsular of Sinai. Many traces of ancient mining operations have been found among the rocks of this district. (*See* BRONZE.)

Coptic. Roughly speaking Coptic is the modern survival of the ancient Egyptian language, and the knowledge of it is invaluable for the study of hieroglyphs. The Coptic characters are modifications of the Greek letters, to which six signs were added from the

ⲚⲈⲢⲱⲨⲠⲞⲨⲤ̄ⲒⲢⲈ ⲌⲨ̄ ⲠⲦⲞⲩⲨⲞⲨⲚ ⲦⲠⲞⲖⲒⲤ

Demotic, in order that those sounds which had no equivalent in Greek could be expressed. There were two dialects—called the " Boheiric," from Bohêra, a province in the Delta, and the " Sahidic," which last was the older and fuller.

Coptos. Greek name for *Qebt*, capital of the fifth nome of Upper Egypt, the modern Kuft. Chief deity, Âmsu. It was one of the most important towns of ancient Egypt, as it was to this town that the trade from Kosseir, on the Red Sea, came.

Cosmetics. Perfumes to give an agreeable smell to the body were much in request, as also different kinds of oils and unguents for rubbing into the skin. "Sweet oil on their heads and on their new head-dresses" was required on great festivals by all who could afford it. Cakes of ointment were placed on the heads of guests at feasts, and to be anointed with the oil of *Qemi* was considered an especial honour. Alabaster pots containing unguent have been found in the tombs. Black and green paint were also in use for the eyes.

Cow. This animal was sacred to Hathor, the goddess who is sometimes represented with a cow's ears, or even the whole head. The cow also represented Nut, the sky goddess (*q.v.*), and at times Isis is also connected with it. In the "Book of the Dead" seven mystic names are given to the divine cow, who is there the wife of the bull Osiris. (*See* MEHURT.)

Crocodile. In old times there were innumerable crocodiles in the Nile, and the Egyptians went out to hunt them. But there are no representations on tomb-walls of this hunting, possibly because of religious scruples, as the animal was sacred to Sebek (*q.v.*). The animal is often depicted in the water beneath boats, and some scenes show him seized by a hippopotamus.

Crocodilopolis. Anciently called *Shed*. It was the capital of a province of the Fayûm known as *Ta-she*, "the land of the Lake," probably a reference to Lake Moeris.

Crown. ⟨hieroglyphs⟩ are the crowns most frequently seen on the monuments. The head-dress formed an important and significant part of the king's royal uniform, and many are the varieties of crown pictured

upon tomb and temple walls. The festival crown
seems to have been the *Pschent* (No. 7), which was
a combination of the white crown of Upper Egypt
(No. 4) and the red crown of Lower Egypt (No. 6).
On warlike occasions and even in times of peace,
the king is seen wearing the *Khepersh* (No. 3) or
war helmet. The "keeper of the king's diadem"
held a high position at court under the Old Empire;
but the office was done away with during the New
Empire. The gods are always depicted as wearing
crowns, and many of them are most complicated, as
Nos. 15 and 16; No. 18 is one which is frequently seen
on kings as well as gods, it is known as the *Atef* crown.
The queen's head-dress represented a vulture with his
wings spread round her head in the act of protection.

Cubit. This measure of length was approximately
20·6 inches. It varied slightly, however, at different
periods as employed by different architects.

Cusae. The Greek name for *Kes*, the capital of the
fourteenth nome of Upper Egypt, the modern Kusîyeh.
Chief deity, Hathor.

Cynocephalus (*Āāni*). The dog-headed ape, sacred
to Thoth, under which form the god is sometimes
represented. Thoth being a moon
god, the cynocephali are frequently
represented with the lunar disk
on their heads. The Hermopolitan
ennead was sometimes represented
by nine cynocephali, that is, Thoth
and eight other deities; but sometimes the eight apes attend Åmen.
They are called "watchers for
the dawn." Nine cynocephali
were said to open the gates in the

Cynocephalus.

west for the setting sun, and each is then called
by a name : "Opener of the earth," "Soul of the
earth," "Heart of the earth," etc. They are thus

represented in the illustrations to a work frequently inscribed on the walls of royal Theban tombs, relating to the passage of the sun during the hours of night, and called " The book of that which is in the under-world." In the judgment scene represented in papyri of the " Book of the Dead," and on the walls at Dêr el Medineh, a cynocephalus is seated on the balance in the middle of the beam of the scales in which the heart of the deceased is being weighed, while Thoth stands by with palette and reed pen waiting to record the result. In this case the cynocephalus may represent equilibrium, which would naturally be a quality of the god Thoth.

D

Dance. Dancing as a spectacle was a favourite amusement of the old Egyptians, but it is improbable that it was a pastime, at least among the upper classes. The performers were usually women, and the dance would seem to have been more a rhythmic movement than anything involving much energy. Dancing women are usually seen in representations of feasts. They appear also in funeral processions, and in every case are accompanied by music and clapping of the hands.

There were apparently war dances and harvest dances performed by men, which were probably national dances. A picture on a tomb wall at Beni Hasan represents such a war dance.

Darius. *See* PERSIAN DYNASTY.

Decree of Canopus. A stela in the Cairo Museum on which is inscribed in hieroglyphs, demotic, and Greek the decree made at Canopus by the Egyptian priests, in council assembled, concerning the festivals which were to be held in honour of Ptolemy Euergetes and his queen Berenīce. Mention is also made of the great benefits which this ruler had conferred upon the country, and a statement is added requiring that the tri-lingual copy of this inscription shall be set up in every temple in the country.

Delta. The flat alluvial land in Lower Egypt lying between the great arms of the Nile, immediately north of Memphis. This district from its likeness to the Greek letter Δ, received the name of the Delta.

Demons in the modern sense of the word—irredeemably evil spirits—figure largely in Graeco-Egyptian magical papyri in which the greater part of the spells are addressed to demons. Much importance was attached to the names of the demons and their right pronunciation. (*See* MAĀT KHERU.)

Demotic. The name given to a cursive modification of the hieratic (*q.v.*) used for the vulgar dialect; it is not found until the XXVth Dynasty. It was introduced about B.C. 900 and was in use until the fourth century A.D. Composed of the same mixture of signs as the hieratic, it is extremely difficult to decipher, owing partly to

the similarity of signs which have separate hieratic equivalents, and partly to the fact that the writing is thick and careless. Like its parent the hieratic it reads from right to left.

Professor H. Brugsch has published a demotic grammar, but very little advancement is made in the study of the characters, all the work in it being done by a few men. Nor are the subjects of demotic documents as a rule very interesting, since they consist chiefly of contracts of sale and legal matters; some magical texts and a curious tale being the chief exceptions. (Papyrus of Setna in the Cairo Museum. See trans. by Brugsch, Rev. Arch., Sept., 1867, and by F. Ll. Griffith.)

Dêr el Medineh. A small temple begun by Ptolemy IV. and finished by Ptolemy IX. It lies between the Colossi and Medinet Habu. It is specially interesting as containing the only lapidary representation of the Psychostasia (*q.v.*).

Digit. An unit of measurement and like the cubit subject to slight variations. The mean value of its length may be roughly estimated at ·727 inch. Professor Petrie has pointed out that the cubit and the digit " have no integral relation one to the other."

Diodorus Siculus. A Greek historian, whose ponderous work in forty books was written, it is supposed, after the death of Julius Caesar. One section treats of the mythic history of the Egyptians, but its value to students of Egyptology is lessened by the author's evident want of discrimination.

Diospolis. The Greek name for *Pa Khen-en-Ament*, capital of the seventeenth nome of Lower Egypt, the modern Ebshan. Chief deity, Amen Rā.

Diospolis Parva. The Greek name for *Het*, capital of the seventh nome of Upper Egypt, the modern Hou. Chief deity, Hathor.

Dog. This animal was used for hunting in the desert, and was occasionally made a pet. The hunting dog was of the nature of a greyhound, with pointed upright ears and curly tail. The *Slughi*, used now-a-days for the same purpose in the Sudan, seem to be a survival of this dog. Tomb pictures of the Old Empire show them attacking antelopes, and even lions were not too big-game for them. Three different breeds of dogs are pictured in XIth Dynasty tombs, one being long-bodied, short-legged and prick-eared. They are sometimes shown under their master's chair, or by his side.

Dolls. *See* Toys.

Donkey. This animal is frequently depicted on the tomb walls, sometimes in small droves. It was much used as a beast of burden. One picture of an ass and her foal shows the creature as heavily laden as one may see them now-a-days. Plutarch states that the ass was abhorred by the Egyptians, but nothing has been discovered to corroborate this theory. A chapter in the " Book of the Dead " is curiously named " the Chapter of repulsing the eater of the Ass," the accompanying vignettes showing "the eater" to be a serpent.

Doors. No temple or house doors remain from ancient times, but the sockets and places for hinges are frequently seen in doorways of tombs and temples. The " doors " of the pyramids consisted of huge blocks of granite let into place after the body was deposited, effectually closing and concealing the entrance. As wood was extremely valuable in Egypt, it is probable that whenever a fixed door was not necessary for the sake of security, hangings were allowed to do duty in the doorways. Texts speak of temple doors made of wood and incrusted with precious metals.

Dreams. There is sufficient evidence to show that dreams were considered of no little importance. They were looked upon as " revelations from a world quite as real as that which we see about us when waking " (Renouf). They were sent by the gods and were much desired, even magic being resorted to to produce them. Formulae for coercing the gods to send

certain dreams have been found, but they are of a late
date. Prophetic dreams sometimes required explana-
tion by a professional expert, of whom there was a
recognized class, the Hersheshta, lasting until Greek
times. Among instances of dreams in Egyptian lore
are :—(*a*) that recorded on the tablet in front of the
Sphinx, in which Thothmes IV. tells how the god
(Harmakhis) appeared to him and made him many
promises on condition that he cleared away the sand
from around his image, i.e. the Sphinx; (*b*) the
Sallier Papyrus II. gives the counsels of Åmen-em-ḥāt
I. to his son, which were revealed to that son in a
dream; (*c*) it was in a dream that the Prince of
Bekhten was visited by the god Khensu and ordered
to return his statue to Thebes (see story of the
possessed princess of Bekhten, on a stela in the
Bibliothèque Nationale); (*d*) an Ethiopian stela records
how the Pharaoh had a dream which was interpreted
to him to mean that he would unite Egypt and Ethiopia
under one sceptre; (*e*) the dream of the Pharaoh
which was interpreted by Joseph in Genesis xli.

Dyeing. From the fact that the Egyptians dyed
linen, as well as wool, we know that they understood
the use of mordants. It is to this process of preparing
the materials to receive the dye that Pliny refers,
when he says, "There exists in Egypt a wonderful
method of dyeing. The white cloth is stained in
various places, not with dye stuffs, but with substances
which have the property of absorbing (fixing) colours.
These applications are not visible upon the cloth; but
when the pieces are dipped into a hot cauldron containing the dye, they are drawn out an instant after dyed.
The remarkable circumstance is, that though there be
only one dye in the vat, yet different colours appear
on the cloth; nor can the colours be afterwards
removed. A vat which would of itself only confuse
the colours on cloth previously dyed, in this way
imparts several colours from a single dye stuff, painting
as it boils."

Dynasties. " Manetho of Sebennytos, who wrote a history of Egypt for the use of Alexandrine Greeks, adopted, on some unknown authority, a division of thirty-one dynasties from Menes to the Macedonian conquest, and his system has prevailed—not, indeed on account of its excellence, but because it is the only complete one which has come down to us."

These Dynasties were grouped together by Lepsius into three great divisions, usually called—the **Ancient Empire**, Dynasties I.—XI.; the **Middle Empire**, Dynasties XII.—XVII.; the **New Empire**, Dynasties XVIII.—XXXI.

	DYNASTIES.	NAME.	DURATION.
ANCIENT EMPIRE.	I.—II.	Thinite	555 Years.
	III.—V.	Memphite . . .	746 ,,
	VI.	Elephantiné . . .	203 ,,
	VII.—VIII.	Memphite . . .	{ 142 ,, { 70 Days.
	IX.—XI.	Heracleopolite . . .	294 Years.
MIDDLE EMPIRE.	XII.—XIII.	Theban	666 ,,
	XIV.	Xoïte	184 ,,
	XV.—XVII.	Hyksos (Delta) . .	511 ,,
NEW EMPIRE.	XVIII.—XX.	Theban	593 ,,
	XXI.	Tanite	130 ,,
	XXII.	Bubastite	170 ,,
	XXIII.	Tanite	89 ,,
	XXIV.	Saïte	6 ,,
	XXV.	Ethiopian . . .	50 ,,
	XXVI.	Saïte	138 ,,
	XXVII.	Persian	121 ,,
	XXVIII.	Saïte	7 ,,
	XXIX.	Mendesian . . .	21 ,,
	XXX.	Sebennyte . . .	38 ,,
	XXXI.	Persian	8 ,,

E

Eileithyias. The city of Lucina, capital of the third nome of Upper Egypt, the modern El-Kab, and the site of a very ancient city, the oldest objects dating back to Dynasty VI. The goddess Nekhebt was worshipped there.

Electron. An amalgam consisting of two-fifths gold and three-fifths silver.

Elephantiné. The Greek name for the capital of *Ab*, the first nome of Upper Egypt, an island opposite to the modern Aswân. The chief deity worshipped there was Khnemu.

Embalming. According to Herodotus the most elaborate and expensive process cost £250. A body thus mummified came through the following processes :—First, an incision was made in the side,—the operator being ceremonially chased away, —and the viscera removed (*see* CANOPIC JARS). The cavity thus made was cleansed with palm wine and filled with myrrh, cassia, &c. The brain was removed through the nostrils by means of a bent instrument. The incision sewn up, the body was placed in a bath of natron for seventy days. At the end of this period it was washed, and swathed in innumerable gummed bandages. Amulets were placed now and again under the bandages, and on the breast a scarabaeus. Finally, a canvas shroud was kept in place by four or five broader bandages. Chapters from the "Book of the Dead" were sometimes written on the wrappings.

In a less expensive method, costing about £90, the abdomen was injected with "cedar tree pitch," which Herodotus states "had a corrosive and solvent action on the viscera." The contents were afterwards allowed to escape. The natron bath was common to every method, the bodies of the poorest being prepared for it by simply rinsing the abdomen with " smyrnaea."

Enchorial; another name for DEMOTIC (*q.v.*).

Ennead. A cycle of nine deities, of whom one was chief and the others his assistants. This cycle represents sometimes the entire Egyptian Pantheon and at others the gods of the particular locality. The most important was the Heliopolitan ennead. It consisted of Tum-Rā as chief, Shu and Tefnut, their children Seb and Nut, and their grandchildren Osiris, Isis, Set and Nephthys; but the gods of the enneads were not always thus related to one another.

Epagomenal Days. The five days which were added to the old Egyptian year of twelve months of thirty days, in order to bring it to the length of the true year. The legend was that Thoth had invented them for the convenience of Nut. For that goddess having fallen into the embraces of Seb, was cursed by her husband Rā, who swore that on no day of any year should she bring forth her children; but by the invention of these days she was rescued from her predicament. (*See* YEAR.)

Esneh. The Egyptian *S-net;* the Greek Latopolis, so called because its inhabitants were said to have worshipped the latus fish. The remains of the temple are of the Roman period, though Thothmes III. originally built one here.

Evil Eye. There is distinct evidence that this superstition existed among the old Egyptians. There is a record of a book stored in the library of the temple of Dendera which treated of the turning away of the evil eye. A favourite woman's name was Stau-ar-ban, which means " she who turns away the evil eye."

"**Eye of Horus**." "An expression denoting any God-sent gift." (Erman.)

Eye, the Sacred. The sacred eye, or the eye of Rā, or heaven, is the sun, a poetic symbolism used by poets throughout time, "heaven's eye" being a frequent Shakesperian phrase. Horus says, "I am he who resides in the middle of the eye." But there are usually two eyes represented, and called the eyes of Horus, a left and a right. They sometimes represent, the right the sun, and the left the moon; but some other meaning must be inferred when it is said of Rā, "Thou openest *the two eyes* and earth is flooded with rays of light." When Rā says "Call unto me mine eye," he refers to the goddess Sekhet (*q.v.*). Another text speaks of Kadesh as the "eye of Rā," and "eye of Tum." The Egyptian word for this eye is *Uzat* or *Utchat* (*q.v.*), which signifies "the healthy" or "flourishing."

F

Festival Songs of Isis and Nephthys. A work probably not older than the XXVIth Dynasty; the author is unknown. It forms part of the funeral hieratic papyrus of Nesi Ámsu (*q.v.*) (No. 10158 in the British Museum). The title is "The Verses of the Festival of the two Zerti," and the papyrus tells us it was to be sung by two virgins in the temple of Osiris on the occasion of the annual festival held for five days in the fourth month of the sowing season. There is evidence in the text that other copies existed, and that it was old enough to allow of variant readings having crept in. With the "Litanies of Seker," which follows, consisting of four columns, it occupies twenty-one of the thirty-three columns of the whole papyrus. The second composition, which was evidently intended to be sung after the Festival Verses, consists of three parts: I. A Litany to the Sun-God; II. A Recitation by Isis; III. A Litany to the Hathors. During the sixteen repetitions of it which were required, it was to have an accompaniment of tambourines.

A hieratic papyrus of Berlin contains a work very similar to the "Festival Songs." It has been translated by M. de Horrack, and is entitled "Les Lamentations d'Isis et Nephthys" (*q.v.*).

"The subject of the verses throughout is the destruction of Osiris by Set, and the reconstruction of his body by Isis and Nephthys."

Festivals. Innumerable festivals were held during the year in honour of various gods. Harvest festivals were held in honour of the god MIN. Part of the year was devoted to those held in honour of Osiris, at the end of which, on the 30th of the month *Khoiak*, a strange festival was held at Busiris to commemorate the setting up of the backbone of the god. A mock fight was then carried on between priests of different sanctuaries, possibly symbolizing the fight between Set and Osiris. Perhaps the most universally acknowledged of all the festivals were those in honour of HĀPI the Nile god, and OSIRIS. Those of HATHOR seem to have taken a somewhat bacchanalian form. Inscriptions tell of an "Intoxication festival" in her honour held at Dendera. At Saïs the festivals were principally dedicated to NEITH. At Memphis that of PTAH-SEKER-OSIRIS was celebrated with great pomp; it fell on December 22nd in late times, and was connected with the winter solstice. A hymn to Amen-Rā speaks of the festival of the quarter month, and of the 6th and 9th days of the month. For every act of importance to the people in the year there was a special festival, the cutting of the dyke, opening the canals, reaping the first sheaf, carrying the corn, and so on. On great festival occasions the image or symbol of the god or goddess was carried in its special bark round the temple and about the precincts. There was, as well, the festival for the dead on the 17th of Thoth, called also the fire festival, when the priests kindled fires in front of the statues in the sepulchral chambers, and the whole country lighted new lamps, and spent the night in feasting and visiting. One of the most important of the festivals was that which took place on the 1st of Thoth (i.e. the early days of August) on the day of the rising of Sothis (Sirius), which marked the beginning of a new year.

Fish. The fish are among the best drawn animals on tomb and temple walls. Hence it is that ichthyologists have been able to identify the fish represented on the walls of Dêr el Baḥri with modern Red Sea fish. Of the many specimens that were found in the Nile several were considered good for food, among which Gardiner Wilkinson gives *Labrus Niloticus*, *perca nilotica*, *cyprinus benni*, *silurus shall*, *silurus schilbe niloticus*, *silurus bajad*, *silurus carmuth*. Some were considered sacred in different parts of the country. Such were the oxyrhinchus, the latus, the phagrus, and the lepidotus. The two former gave their names to places. That fishing was a great industry, as well as one of the chief sports and amusements, may be gathered from the pictures on tomb walls. Nets of various kinds, hooks, and spears were used for catching fish. It is evident that they were preserved and fed for the table in private ponds, and here the Egyptian gentleman amused himself by fishing with a line, or going out in a small boat to spear the fish with a bident. The ordinary fisherman, who fished for his livelihood, used a net ; a drag net is often worked by two boats. The fish thus caught were eaten both fresh and salted. The latter were split and opened out, exposing the backbone, salted, and hung out in the sun. Herodotus speaks of "the revenue arising from Lake Moeris, which was derived from the fish," and alluding to the subsiding of the waters of the inundation from Lake Moeris he says, "During the six months that it flows out it yields a talent of silver every day to the king's treasury from the fish, but when the water is flowing into it, twenty minae." In later times fish was considered an impure food, and was not eaten by the priests.

Flora. That the Egyptians had a great love for flowers is a very evident fact, since they figure at every function and on every occasion. But their choice was limited. The trees and plants in old times were probably very much the same as those we see now. The date and dôm palms, the sycomore and the acacia were the only big trees, and the lotus and mimosa were apparently the only flowers that grew in abundance. The papyrus was largely grown. Wheat, barley and dhurra were the chief crops. Of vegetables there was no lack, though variety seems to have been limited to onions and cucumbers of different kinds. Melons and grapes, dates, figs and pomegranates were the chief fruits used.

Fortifications. The two most celebrated lines of fortification are the one line in the Delta, made during the M.E., the ruins of which are still standing. It consists of a long wall strengthened at intervals by small forts or migdols; the other is in Nubia, commanding the desert roads to the Red Sea, to Berber, and to Gebel Barkal, on the Upper Nile. (*See* FORTRESSES.)

Fortresses. From the earliest days the Egyptians erected fortresses against the incursions of the Asiatics, Bedawîn, and Nubians. The most ancient are those of Abydos and El-Kab. In the Delta a line of forts was erected under the M.E., and called the "gates of the barbarians." Above Aswân, on the Nubian frontier, was a fortress called the "gate of the south,"

which was commanded sometimes by the nomarch of
Thebes, and sometimes by the " superintendent of the
South." At Semneh and Kummeh, in Nubia, just
above the second cataract, Usertsen III.(Dynasty XII.),
erected two great forts immediately opposite to each
other, to bar the water-way against the southern tribes.
Most of the cities of ancient Egypt were strongly
fortified—notably Thebes, Ombos, On, Sân and Saïs.
El-Kab, the ruins of which are still standing, is the
oldest walled city in Egypt. The ruins of many other
fortresses are still in existence.

Foundation Deposits. The chief finds have been at
the following places :—Naukratis ; at the four corners
of the great temenos, and two smaller ones at the
corners of the central hall.—Illahun ; on the site of a
ruined pyramid, five pits.—Tell Defenneh ; at the four
corners of a fort.—Tell Nebesheh ; at the N.E. and S.E.
corners of a " destroyed limestone building ;" also at
three corners, (not N.E.) and centre, of a temple built
by Åahmes II. of the XXVIth Dynasty.—Gemaiyemi ;
at three corners, (not N.E.) and centre of a building.
—Dêr-el-Bahri ; beneath the temple of Hatshepsut.—
Kahun ; in the centre of area of temple built by
Usertsen II., a hole 31 ins. sq. by 4 feet deep, four
sets of objects.—Alexandria ; a Ptolemaic find. A
gold plate with an inscription recording the foundation of the temenos at Kanobos to Osiris, is also of the
Ptolemaic period.

The pits in which the deposits were placed were
usually closed by one slab of stone, or, as at Illahun, by
two slabs with sand between. The objects deposited
were : plaques of gold, silver, lead, copper, carnelian,
green felspar, lapis lazuli, jaspar, terra-cotta, and
enamelled ware ; pottery of various kinds, some
evidently ceremonial imitations of larger ones ; mortars ;
corn-rubbers ; bones of sacrificial animals ; libation
cups ; specimens of various ores ; mud bricks ; strings of
carnelian beads. At Tukh-el-Karmus thirty-two blue
porcelain saucers formed part of the deposit. In the

four deposits at the temenos of Naukratis were sixty-eight objects. In later deposits there are no carnelian beads; but the model tools and corn-rubbers are still present. (*See* memoirs of the Egypt Exploration Fund.)

Frog. *See* AMULETS.

Funerary Cones. Rough terra cotta cones about ten inches high and three inches across, with horizontal lines of inscription on the base, which were usually coloured. The inscription gives the name of the deceased. Various theories have been proposed as to the probable use of these objects, but it is most likely that they were models of loaves or cakes that were placed in the tomb, and neither seals, architectural ornaments nor marks for sepulchral sites.

G

Games. The games that have been pictured on tomb walls have their analogies in modern ones. Odd and even, *mora*, and draughts are the most frequent. Shooting with arrows at a mark, throwing javelins at a block of wood and a form of "la gràce" also occur. Many draught-boards and men have been found, but it is impossible to recover the rules of the game or to know the way in which it was played. It is evident from the variety of boards discovered that there were many ways. *Mora* is the name given now in Italy to a game also played by the old Romans, which consists in one person suddenly holding up a certain number of fingers for an instant, the other player having to guess the number. Games played with dice belong to late times. (*See* SPORTS.)

Gardens. A garden was one of the most expensive luxuries of the wealthy, owing to the necessity for perpetual irrigation. There are several pictures, or plans, of gardens on tomb walls. They show rows of trees and shrubs, one, two, or more ponds with water-plants, fish and a boat, vines on trellises, and small kiosques.

Glass. The manufacture of glass was early known to the Egyptians, but they never could make it quite white and absolutely transparent, from their inability to eliminate certain chemical substances. It has always a greenish tinge. The manufacture was not an exact science, their chemistry was empirical, and the results uncertain. Strabo was told in Alexandria that Egypt possessed an "earth" which was peculiarly suitable for the manufacture of glass. Possibly this "earth" was soda, for in the middle ages we find the Venetians importing soda from Alexandria for the purpose of glass manufacture. On early tomb walls are seen men working glass with a blow-pipe. Glass was employed for vessels of many shapes, and also very largely for enamelling. In rare cases inscriptions cut in the wooden sarcophagi were filled in with it. Beakers, figurines, amulets and beads were made of it.

Gold. In the hieroglyphs ⌐ᵐᵐᵐ⌐. It was in common use in Egypt, vases, cups, ingots, plaques and rings being depicted on the monuments. The rings may be seen in scales, being weighed, doubtless a substitute for coinage, of which the ancient Egyptians had no know-ledge. The gold was obtained from the so-called "Arabian desert," that is, the country between the Nile and the Red Sea, where the veins of quartz in the mountains contain gold, and from Nubia. The inscriptions speak of different qualities, such as "mountain gold," "gold of twice," "gold of thrice," &c. Gilding, or "overlaying with gold" was largely practised, objects in stone, wood, and other materials as well as the heads of mummies being thus decorated,

Even scarabs of lapis lazuli were sometimes gilded. (*See* JEWELLERY.)

Granaries. Large chambers built of brick and standing in a row of ten or twelve. They were oven-shaped and had no communication with each other. The corn was poured in through an opening at the top and removed through a small door at the bottom. The granaries were kept carefully guarded, and were under the care of the " Superintendent of the Granaries."

Granite, or Syenite, from *Syene*, i.e. Aswân, whence it was most extensively quarried, is found in great variety in Egypt. There are pink and red syenites, porphyritic granite, yellow, grey, black, and white kinds; and others veined with white or with black are to be found within a small area round the first cataract. Granite was largely used in all its varieties in the building of temples, the making of royal sarcophagi, colossi, obelisks, tabernacles, official stelae and statues. The finer grained kinds were even used for small objects such as amulets. The principal pyramids were originally partly cased in this material.

H

Hair Restorer. There are several prescriptions in the Ebers Medical Papyrus which are said to be sure remedies for baldness, and for restoring hair to the original colour after it had turned white. Queen Shesh, the mother of King Teta, of the VIth Dynasty, found an excellent remedy for the falling out of her hair in the following pomade, made of the hoof of a donkey, a dog's pad and some date kernels, which were to be all boiled together in oil. Another sovereign remedy was to be found in the use of the plant *Degem*. To

prevent the hair from becoming white or to restore it
to its youthful colour, a remedy could be made of " the
blood of a black calf that had been boiled in oil."
" The blood of the horn of a black bull " boiled in oil
and made into an ointment was also useful for the
same purpose. The " fat of a black snake " was also
thought to produce excellent results. It was equally
possible to cause the hair of a " hated rival " to fall
out, for which purpose it was necessary to boil together
in oil the flower *sepet* and a particular kind of worm,
and get it put on the head of the rival. Against this,
however, there was an antidote in the fat of the
hippopotamus, with which a boiled tortoiseshell had
been pounded up, but then the head must be anointed
" very, very often."

Hamḥit.

Hamḥit. A goddess spoken of on the
stela of Mendes as " Hamḥit the powerful
one of Mendes, the wife of the god in the
temple of the ram, the eye of the sun, the
lady of heaven, queen of all the gods."
She is represented with a fish on her head.

Hāp. Name of the sacred bull at
Memphis. (*See* Apis.)

Hāpi.

Hāpi. The Nile deified
under the form of a human
figure, partly male and partly
female. In his hands are
sometimes seen a table of
offerings upon which are
lotus flowers and libation vases, while
on his head is a bunch of lotus flowers.

Hāpi. One of the four sons of Horus,
the funerary genii who also represent
the four cardinal points, and were protectors of the four canopic jars (*q.v.*). He
is represented with the head of a cynocephalus. (*See* Amset.)

Harem. The Harem in the modern Turkish sense of the word did not exist in old times. Some of the Pharaohs had several wives; but it seems quite incompatible with the language in which the "mistress of the house" is spoken of, that the practice of polygamy and concubinage should have been common. A few instances occur in which we find records of men with two wives.

Harmakhis. The Egyptian *Hor - em - Khuti* or *Hormakhu*, "Horus of the two horizons." He is more especially the rising sun, and as such was represented by the great Sphinx on the pyramid plateau. He is also called Rā-Harmakhis as god of Heliopolis. He is always depicted with a hawk's head and usually with the disk and uraeus. (*See* HORUS.)

Harmakhis.

Haroëris. The Greek name for a form of Horus, called in Egyptian "the elder," and son of one form of Hathor. He was worshipped at Letopolis (*q.v.*), and the double temple at Kom Ombo was dedicated partly to him and partly to Sebek. In later times he was said to be a son of Rā. (*See* HORUS.)

Harp. This instrument was in use in Egypt from the earliest times, many varieties being depicted on the tomb walls. Sometimes it was played alone, sometimes with other instruments, and sometimes as an accompaniment to the voice. The number of strings varied from four to twenty-two. Some were of great size, the musician standing to play. More often he sat on his heels on the ground. The instrument either rested on the ground or was sup

Harper.

ported by a kind of prop. It was often ornamented with elaborate designs in colours. (*See* HARPER, LAY OF THE.)

Harper; Lay of the. A chant or song " that is written before the harper," which is inscribed on the walls of two tombs at Thebes and transcribed in the Harris Papyrus. It is not a religious chant, but rather a moralizing poem in the strain of the Scriptural Ecclesiastes. One version ends thus:

" For no one carries away his goods with him,
Yea no one returns again who has gone thither."

A translation may be found in " Records of the Past," vol. iv.

Harpocrates. The Greek name for Horus, son of Isis, and the avenger of his father Osiris. He is always represented in human form, and usually with his finger to his mouth.

Hatasu. *See* HATSHEPSUT.

Hathor. One of the most important goddesses of the Egyptian Pantheon. Her name signifies "the House of Horus," and in one aspect she is a sky goddess, Horus the sun rising and setting in her. Her best known form is as the goddess of beauty, love, and joy. As such she was in later times identified by the Greeks with their Aphrodite. Many festivals were held in her honour, and the great temple at Dendera was devoted to her

Harpocrates.

cult. In another form she is the "Lady of the Underworld." The cow was her sacred animal, she herself being sometimes represented in the form of a cow. More often she is shown as a woman, though sometimes wearing the cow's head or ears. Her characteristic headdress is the disk between two horns. Nearly all goddesses were at times identified with her, and when this happens they usually wear her attributes, the disk and horns. Very frequently Hathor is represented suckling Horus.

Hathor.

Hatshepsut, Queen, *Maāt-ka-Rā*, Dynasty XVIII.,

B.C. 1516—1481. This queen was the daughter and heiress of Thothmes I., and was married to her half-brother, Thothmes II., by whom she had two daughters, Neferu-Rā, who died young, and Hatshepset, who became the wife of Thothmes III.

Hatshepsut is one of the most interesting figures in Egyptian history. Left a widow quite young, she took up the reins of government with vigour and decision, and during her reign raised the country to a most prosperous condition. Apparently she preferred the arts of peace to the conquest of fresh territory. Her name will be remembered for all time by the magnificent and unique temple of Dêr-el-Baḥri, built under the Theban hills. Its great historic interest lies in the representation upon one of the dividing walls of the expedition to the land of Punt. This purely commercial and pacific expedition was ostensibly to seek for and bring back some of the incense trees which did not grow in Egypt. Hatshepsut's envoys were successful, and besides returning with some of the precious trees, which were planted in the garden of Åmen, they brought to their queen the allegiance of the people of Punt, and rich gifts of electron, ebony, ivory, leopard skins, incense, and wild animals. At Karnak she erected two obelisks, the greater one being to celebrate the *Sed* festival, in the sixteenth year of her reign. It is nearly 100 ft. high, and is cut out of red granite; it was quarried at Aswân, inscribed, polished, and set up in its place in the incredibly short period of seven months.

Hawk. This bird was sacred to Horus, and was frequently mummified. If any deity is represented with the head of a hawk it may be safely concluded that he was one of the solar gods.

Heh or **Hehu.** The god of eternity. He is represented with the head of a frog. A feminine form, Heht, is shown with different heads, sometimes a uraeus, sometimes a sheep, or a cat.

Heken. A form of Ta-urt represented with the body of a hippopotamus and the head of a vulture.

Heqt. The frog-headed goddess, the mother of *Haroëris* (*q.v.*), and sometimes spoken of as the wife of *Khnemu.* Her rôle is rather vague, but it is evident that she was associated with the idea of the resurrection, and her symbol, the frog, was carried on into Christian times, being often found upon terra-cotta lamps.

Heqt.

Heliopolis. The Greek name for *Ånnu* capital of the thirteenth nome of Lower Egypt, near the modern Matarîyeh. The chief deity was Râ, the sun god, from which fact the Greek name comes. It was the Scriptural On, whence Joseph took his wife. (*See* ÅNNU.)

Hennu. The sacred boat which was drawn through the temples at dawn. (*See* BARKS.)

Henotheism. "A phase of religious thought, in which the individual gods invoked are not conceived as limited by the power of others." (Renouf.)

"Each god is to the mind of the suppliant as good as all other gods. He is felt at the time as a real divinity, as supreme and absolute in spite of the necessary limitations which to our mind a plurality of gods must entail on every single god. All the rest disappear from the vision . . . and he only who is to fulfil their desires stands in full light before the eyes of the worshippers." (Max Müller.)

Hermes Trismegistos. "Hermes thrice great" was the author of several works, of which only fragments remain. Much mystery attaches to his name. The Greeks had adopted the Egyptian god Thoth into their pantheon under the name of Hermes. According to Clemens Alexandrinus, Thoth wrote forty-two books, the latest of which probably dates from the XXVIth Dynasty. But only very small parts of these works remain in the writings of Stobaeus and others of that time. These again have been claimed by some authorities as post-Christian, because of their similarity to the works of Neo-platonic writers.

Heracleopolis Magna. Greek name for *Seten henen*, the capital of the twentieth nome of Upper Egypt, the modern Ahnasieh. Chief deity, Hershefi.

Heptanomis. A district of Middle Egypt, consisting of seven nomes and the oases, lying between the Thebaïd and the Delta.

Her-hor. Dynasty XXI., circa B.C. 1100.

The chief priest of Amen at the end of the XXth Dynasty, who wrested the throne from the effete Ramessides, and proclaimed himself " king of Upper and Lower Egypt." His power, strictly speaking, was limited to the Thebaïd and Ethiopia.

Hermonthis. The Greek name for *Annu qemāt*, the " Southern On," capital of the fourth nome of Upper Egypt, the modern Karnak. Chief deity, Mentu, the war god.

Hermopolis. The Greek name for *Pa-Tehuti*, capital of the fifteenth nome of Lower Egypt, the modern El Bakalîyeh. Chief deity, Thoth (*Tehuti*).

Hermopolis. The Greek name for *Khemennu*, the capital of the fifteenth nome of Upper Egypt, the modern Eshmunên. Chief deity, Thoth.

Herodotus. The second book of Herodotus' history, called "Euterpe," gives a history of Egypt, many statements in which appear extravagant. Much that he has recorded from hearsay is doubtless incorrect, but in the cases where he speaks as an eye-witness he is generally found to be accurate.

Hershefi, *Arsaphes*. A form of Osiris generally represented with a ram's head.

Hesepti. The Egyptian name for the divisions of the country. (*See* NOMES.)

Hesepti. Fifth king of Dynasty I. ; reigned twenty years. He is mentioned in the Medical Papyrus in Berlin. Books 64 and 130 of the " Book of the Dead " are said to date back to his reign.

Het. A name of the chief town of Diospolis Parva, the seventh nome of Upper Egypt.

Het-sekhem. The sacred name of the metropolis of

Diospolis Parva. Hathor and Nephthys were here worshipped.

Hieratic. The cursive form of writing the Egyptian language, and used chiefly on papyri and wooden

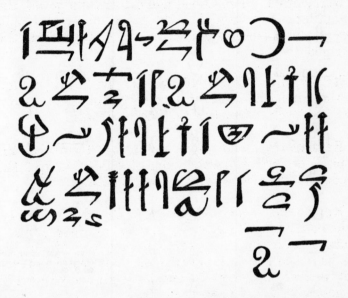

coffins. The characters are usually written from right to left, and very rarely in columns as hieroglyphs are so often engraved. How early hieratic came into use is unknown, but fragments of papyri inscribed with these characters have been found in the ruins of the VIth Dynasty town at Elephantiné. The oldest hieratic document is the Prisse Papyrus (Bibliothèque Nationale, Paris), dating from about the XIth Dynasty. This script was in use until the fourth century A.D.

Hieraconpolis. The Greek name for *Nut-ent-bak*, capital of the twelfth nome of Upper Egypt, the modern Kau el Kebîr. Chief deity, Horus.

Hieroglyphs. The hieroglyphic character employed by the Egyptians was originally pictorial, a form it retained more or less in the case of stone-cut inscriptions until a late date.   The invention of this script

The Alphabet.

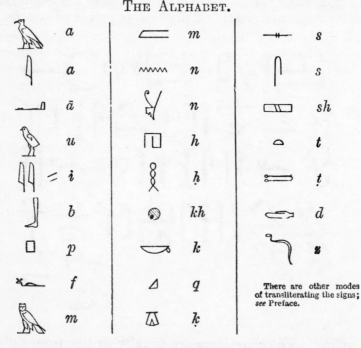

	a		*m*		*s*	
	a		*n*		*s*	
	ā		*n*		*sh*	
	u		*h*		*t*	
	i		*ḥ*		*ṭ*	
	b		*kh*		*d*	
	p		*k*		*ẓ*	
	f		*q*			
	m		*ḳ*			

There are other modes of transliterating the signs; *see* Preface.

was attributed to the god Thoth.   By about 300 A.D. all knowledge of the meaning of the characters had died out, and it was not until the discovery of the Rosetta Stone (*q.v.*) in 1799 that any real progress was made in their decipherment.   We now know that the signs are of two kinds, those representing sounds and those representing ideas—called *phonetic* and *ideographic*.   Of the former, the phonetic characters, there are two kinds, the *alphabetic* and the *syllabic*.   The ideographic signs are pictorial representations of the objects spoken of, which are placed after the phonetically written word to "determine" it, and hence they are *determinatives*.   Determinatives are of two kinds, *generic* and *specific*, the former being determinative of a class—as for instance the picture of the hide of an animal, indicating merely an animal—the latter of a particular object. The texts read either from right to left, or from left to right, or are arranged in columns, there being no rule. The text commences from the side towards which the bird and other animal characters are facing. There are about 500 characters in frequent use. Many of the syllabic signs are polyphonous. The cursive form of the hieroglyphic script is called hieratic (*q.v.*). In later times this cursive form degenerated into a much simpler character called demotic. (*See* SETEN-ḤETEP-TĀ.)

Hipponus. The Greek name for *Ḥet-bennu*, the capital of the eighteenth nome of Upper Egypt, the modern El Hibeh. Chief deity, Anubis.

Hiser. A special name of the Temple of Thoth at Hermopolis.

Ḥit. A form of Bes (*q.v*)., found at Dendera.

Hittites. (*See* KHETA.)

Honey. The Egyptians evidently succeeded in keeping bees, in spite of the scarcity of flowers, for honey enters frequently into their medical recipes. There is some evidence that in late times it was used for preserving the dead.

Hophra. (*See* UAḤ-ÁB-RĀ.)

Ḥor-Ámen. A complex deity, having the attributes of Horus added to those of Ámen. He is represented as Horus, with the side lock and finger to the mouth, and wears the disk and plumes of Ámen.

Horapollo. The author of a fourth century, A.D., work in Greek on hieroglyphs. Nothing is known of the author except that he is called "an Egyptian". It is probable that he was a Copt, and that the original

of his work was written in Coptic, the Greek form
being a translation by one about whom we know
nothing except that his name was Philip.

Horbehutet. The winged disk. He is also represented with two uraei, one on either side of the disk,
which are sometimes depicted wearing the crowns of
Upper and Lower Egypt; they represent the goddesses of the North and South, Uazit and Nekhebt.

Horbehutet was a solar deity who traversed Egypt
with the sun god Rā, warding off evil from him and
conquering his enemies. His symbol was placed over
the gates and chamber doors of the temples to protect
them from destruction. Edfu was the place where
he was honoured as the nome god.

Hor-em-heb, *Rā-ser-kheperu*, XVIIIth Dynasty, cir.

1332-1328 B.C., married Nezem-mut, who was probably the sister of Ámen-hetep IVth's queen. Very
little is known of the reign of this king; and his time
seems to have been chiefly occupied in checking the
abuses that prevailed among the military class.

Hor-merti. (*See* Eyes of Horus.)

Hor-sam-taui. A form of Horus worshipped at
Dendera and Edfu. He is represented as human-
headed.

Hor-shesu, or *Shemsu-heru*. The followers of
Horus who, according to the Turin Papyrus, are sup-

posed to have reigned during the pre-dynastic ages in Egypt for about 13,420 years.

Horse. The horse was unknown in early history. It is represented for the first time on monuments of the XVIIIth Dynasty, and may possibly therefore have been introduced by the Hyksos invaders who preceded this dynasty. In any case horses were an Asiatic importation. They were rarely used for riding, if we judge from the fact that no single representation of an Egyptian on horseback has been found. But one or two texts speak of men on horseback. They were used in large numbers for war chariots, and one papyrus speaks of their being used for ploughing. Appointments in the royal stables were important posts, carrying with them many duties. Ramses II. had two favourite horses, whose names have been recorded. (*See* POEM OF PENTAUR.)

Horus. One of the principal gods of Egypt. Son of Osiris and Isis, he is represented either as a boy or a young man, or with the hawk's head, the last indi-

Horus.

cating his solar aspect. The two forms were two distinct deities in the very earliest times. But the two stories were soon confused, and the Horus who waged war against Set, his father's murderer, became identified with Horus the rising sun, the Greek Apollo. He was worshipped in many forms and under many names throughout Egypt. As a child he was represented with the side lock of hair, and frequently with his finger to his mouth. As a solar deity he figures either as a hawk or a man with a hawk's head, wearing a variety of crowns. As "the sun in his full strength," he is sometimes merged in Rā. (*See* HARMAKHIS, HARPOCRATES, EYES OF HORUS.

Hyksos. A word probably derived from *ḥaq*, a prince, and *Shasu*, the tribes inhabiting the eastern desert. Of the Hyksos—erroneously called Shepherd Kings—very little is known that is absolutely certain. They appear to have been a barbaric people from the east, who, taking advantage of a period of weakness, poured down into Egypt, established their own government, and, after restoring *Ha-uart* (Tanis), governed from Memphis. After 511 years they were expelled from Lower Egypt by Åāḥmes I. and forced into the Delta. Thothmes I. finally expelled them, and they retreated into the country from whence they originally came.

Up to the present time there have only been found the remains of three Hyksos kings, Khian and Åpepi I. and II., under the last of whom it is thought that Joseph served. The genuineness of many of the so-called Hyksos monuments found in museums has been doubted by eminent Egyptologists.

Hymns. Of the number of hymns that have been preserved the greater number are in praise of Rā, the sun-god. But there are also hymns to Ptah, Osiris, the Nile, Åmen, and Hathor. According to Renouf these hymns represent the henotheistic side of Egyptian religion. The ideas expressed in them are often very lofty, and the conception of the Deity is in such language as would be employed in these times. But invariably there is mixed up with these fine passages a great deal of polytheistic teaching. The chief hymns that have been studied are, Hymn to the Nile, in the Sallier Papyrus, translated by Maspero; Hymn to Amen, in a Cairo papyrus, XXth Dynasty, translated by Grébaut; Hymn to Osiris, on a stela in Paris, translated by Chabas; a pantheistic hymn from the temple of El Khargeh, translated by Brugsch, Birch, and Renouf; Hymn to the Aten, in a tomb at Tel el Amarna, translated by Bouriant and Breasted; Hymn to Rā, in the 15th chapter of the "Book of the Dead" (Turin Papyrus), translated by Wiedemann and others. (*See* HENOTHEISM.)

Hypocephalus. A disk of painted linen or of bronze, found under the heads of Graeco-Roman mummies. It is really a form of amulet, and is inscribed with magical formulae and figures of gods—the Hathor cow being invariably among them—and is designed to obtain warmth for the body. An inscription runs round the border of the disk, the other representations being drawn across the field. A scene frequently depicted is one consisting of cynocephalus apes adoring the solar disk in his bark. Part of the border inscription runs as follows: "Chief of the gods, come thou to the Osiris Hor [name of the owner of the hypocephalus] *maāt kheru*. Grant that there be warmth under his head, for he was one of thy followers." (Wiedemann.) Another prayer runs thus: "May the god, who himself is hidden, and whose face is concealed, who shineth upon the world in his forms of existence, and in the underworld, grant that my soul may live for ever. May the great god in his disk give his rays in the underworld of Heliopolis. Grant thou unto me an entrance and an exit in the underworld without let or hindrance." (Budge.)

Hypostyle. The name given to any hall the roof of which is supported by columns, such as the great hypostyle hall at Karnak which was originally roofed over.

Hypselis. The Greek name for *Shâs-ḥetep*, capital of the eleventh nome of Upper Egypt, the modern Shodb. Chief deity, Khnemu.

Human Sacrifice. It remains still a disputed point whether the pylon scenes representing the Pharaoh about to kill his bound enemies indicates the practice of sacrificing the captives to the god after a battle. Nor can it be positively proved that from certain scenes in tombs we are to learn that victims were killed at the death of a rich man in order that their spirits or *kas* (*see* KA) might follow him and minister to him in the other world. If this were so the custom did not survive the civilization of the Theban Empire. M. Maspero has written, " On the occasional persistence of human sacrifice, real or simulated, even into the times of the second Theban Empire."

I

Iamblichus. A Syrian Neo-platonist of the fourth century A.D., to whom has been ascribed the celebrated book " On the Egyptian Mysteries," or " Answer of Âb-Âmen the master to Porphyry's letter to Anebo, and solutions of the doubts therein expressed," a work interesting to the student of Egyptian religion.

Ibis. The bird sacred to Thoth, that god being frequently represented with the head of an ibis. It was the *Ibis Aethiopica*, which is not found north of Wady Halfa. The bird as a hieroglyph forms part of the name of Thoth.

Ideograms. *See* HIEROGLYPHS.

Im-ḥetep. Eighth king of Dynasty IV., cir. 3730 B.C., reigned nine years.

Imḥetep. A god called by the Greeks *Imuthes*, and likened by them to Asklepios. He is the first-born of Ptah, and Nut is his mother. Powers of exorcism and healing were attributed to him. A temple was built to him between the Serapēum and the village of Abusîr. His cult increased in Saïte and Greek times. Statuettes and reliefs represent him as a young man wearing a close cap and often with an open roll of papyrus on his knee.

Imḥetep.

Imuthes. The Greek form of Imḥetep (*q.v.*).

Incubator. "What most excites our wonder, and deserves the greatest praise, is the industry shown by the rearers of fowls and geese, who, not contented with the course of natural procreation known in other countries, hatch an infinite number of birds by an artificial process. Dispensing with the incubation of the hens, they with their own hand bring the eggs to maturity; and the young chickens thus produced are not inferior in any respect to those hatched by natural means." (Diodorus i. 74.)

Ink. *See* PIGMENTS.

Iron. Egypt seems to have had no "iron age" analogous to that of many countries. Examples of the metal are rare until about 800 B.C. The difficulty of obtaining it will account for this, but according to some authorities the metal was held in abhorrence by the Egyptians and was dedicated to Set, which would also account for the few examples found. Moreover, much may have disappeared simply from oxidation. Many iron tools of the Graeco-Egyptian period were obtained during the excavations at Naukratis.

Isis.

Isis. The goddess *Ḥest* or *Áset* is the daughter of Seb and Nut, and wife and sister of Osiris. She is always represented as a woman, and wears on her head the seat or throne ⌡ which is also the hieroglyph for her name. But at times she wears other head-dresses, particularly the vulture cap, the disk and horns, and the double crown. She is the mother of Horus, and as such seems to be merged in Hathor at times. She was the true type of wifehood and motherhood. Her husband Osiris having been killed and his body hidden by Set, she spared no pains in her search to find him, and was aided in her lamentations by her sister Nephthys. It is there-fore, because of every dead person having become an *Osirian*, that these two god-desses are so frequently represented at the head and feet of the mummy in the pictures on tomb walls, and on sarcophagi. With Osiris and Horus, Isis forms one of the best known triads. The great temple at Philae was dedicated to her. In the legend of Rā she figures as a magician ; and she is called also the " great enchantress."

Isis.

Israel Stela. A block of black syenite, measuring
10ft. 3in. high, 5ft. 4in. across, and 13in. thick, found
by Petrie in the ruins of a temple of Mer-en-Ptah at
Thebes. It was used in the first place by Åmen-ḥetep
III, who inscribed on it a record of his religious
benefactions to the temple of Åmen. His son, Akh-
en-Åten, erased a great part of it, particularly the
names of Amen; but the inscription was restored by
Seti I. Mer-en-Ptah took the stone and built it into
his temple with the inscribed face to the wall. Then
on the blank side he carved a long account of his
defeat of the Libyan invaders, followed by a record of
a Syrian campaign, with an enumeration of various
tribes and peoples. Among them occurs a name which
is thought by some to refer to the Israelites of the
Bible. The passage runs as follows :—" Vanquished
are the Tahennu; the Kheta (Hittites) are quieted;
ravaged is Pa-Kanana with all violence; taken is
Askadni (Askelon?); seized is Kazmel; Yenu of the
Syrians is made as though it had not existed; the
people of Ysiraal is spoiled, it hath no seed; Syria has
become as widows of the land of Egypt; all lands
together are in peace." The stela is in the Cairo
museum. The name I-s-r-a-e-l-u has been found on
another stela of the time of Mer-en-Ptah, and identified
by Spiegelberg. It is in the Cairo Museum.

Ithyphallic god. *See* ÅMSU.

Ivory. Though no great number of ivory objects
has been found, we know that the elephant was well-
known from the earliest times, since the animal figures
as a hieroglyph in the name of Elephantiné as far back
as the Vth Dynasty. The perishable nature of the
material probably accounts for the small number of the
finds. It was used for inlaying furniture, and for small
objects, such as spoons, ornaments, combs, dice, and
castanets; boomerangs of ivory have also been found.
Occasionally it was dyed red or green, and sometimes
it was engraved with the point and filled in with black.

Hands and arms of ivory have been found laid on the breasts of mummies. In 1898 Quibell, in the course of his excavations at Nekhen, opposite to El Kab, found several figurines and other objects in ivory.

J

Jewellery. A considerable amount of jewellery has been found, the greater part of it in the form of beads of carnelian, turquoise, lazuli, amethyst, etc., and faïence, which were arranged in necklaces. The custom of burying ornaments on the mummy has preserved to us many fine examples of the jeweller's work, the best of which may be seen in the Cairo Museum. The work of the New Empire was very fine, as the beautiful gold and inlaid work of the bracelets, collars, and pectoral of Queen Áāh-ḥetep show, but is almost surpassed by that of the ornaments of the XIIth Dynasty found at Dahshur. The *cloisons* of gold are filled with carnelian, turquoise, lapis lazuli and other precious stones, instead of paste, though that also was used. More recently, wonderful bracelets of cast and chased gold, and amethyst and lazuli beads have been found at Abydos, which are thought to have belonged to the queen of Zer, of the Ist Dynasty. (*See* RINGS.)

Judgment. *See* PSYCHOSTASIA.

K

Ka. The Ka in Egyptian pneumatology was one of the seven parts of man. It corresponds to the *genius* of classic writers, constituting a separate entity, a kind of spiritual double, as the Fravashis of the Zoroastrians. "As the Roman appeased his genius, so is the Egyptian king frequently sculptured in the act of propitiating his own Ka." The prayers in the tombs are for oblations to the Ka of the deceased. In the earliest times we find mention of the office of *ḥen ka,*

Ka figure.   Ka banner.

i.e. minister or priest of the Ka. In birth scenes, as in that of Ḥatshepsut at Dêr-el-Baḥri there are always two little figures represented, one that of the royal infant, the other his Ka. That the ordinary Egyptian found some little difficulty in so entirely abstract a conception is evidenced by the fact that he made statues for the Ka to inhabit when the body was dead and mummified. These were exact likenesses of the deceased, and one or more were placed in a serdāb (*q.v.*) in the tomb for the use of the Ka. Each king had a special Ka name enclosed in a kind of square cartouche on a banner. It was not only human beings who had Kas but everything, gods, localities, furnishings, and in order that the Ka might be well served, objects he might be supposed to want were broken to free their Kas, and placed in the tomb. The idea is almost equivalent to Paracelsus' theory of astral bodies. (See SETEN-ḤETEP-TĀ.)

Kabasos. Greek name for *Ḥebes-ka*, capital of the eleventh nome of Lower Egypt, the modern Horbeit. The chief deity was Isis.

Kadesh. A goddess, "Lady of Heaven, governess of all gods, the eye of Rā, there exists no second to her." She was one of a group of foreign divinities introduced into Egypt at the time of Dynasty XVIII. She was probably a Phoenician deity, and synonymous with Astarte.

Ka-ka-u, second king of Dynasty II., reigned thirty-nine (?) years. He is said to have established the worship of the Apis bulls at Memphis, the Mnevis bulls at Ánnu (Heliopolis), and the sacred rams at Mendes. (*See* APIS.)

Kamit. The ancient name of Egypt, which means the "black land."

Khat. The corruptible, dead body, symbolized by the ideogram of a dead fish. This body it was necessary to embalm in order to preserve it from decay, so that it might in the future become a *sāhu* or glorified and incorruptible body, possessed of knowledge and power. The Khat probably stands to the *sāhu* in the same relation that the σῶμα σαρκός does to the σῶμα πνευματικός. (*See* SĀHU.)

Khâf-Râ  the Khephren of the

Greeks, third king of the IVth Dynasty. His pyramid
stands between those of Khufu and Men-kau-Râ at
Gizeh. Inscriptions say little of this Pharaoh, but
his features are well known to us from the fine green
diorite statue discovered by M. Mariette at the bottom
of a pit in a temple near the Sphinx. The splendid
workmanship of this statue indicates a very advanced
state of art. There were several other statues in the
same place, but all, having been thrown in, were
broken. Fragments of inscriptions tell us that the
name of Khâf-Râ's wife was Meri-s-anch. (*See*
PYRAMIDS.) The red granite temple usually, but
erroneously, called the Temple of the Sphinx was
probably built by this monarch.

Khaib, the. The shadow of a man or woman, which
left the body at death to continue elsewhere a separate
entity of its own. It is represented under the form of
a sunshade.

Khem. (*See* AMSU.)

Khensu or **Khonsu.** The third
god in the Theban triad, the son
of Amen and Mut. He is a lunar
deity, and as such is confused, and
sometimes, as at Edfu, identified
with Thoth. He occasionally
assumed a solar character, and
is then represented with a hawk-
head, and was emblematic of the
rising sun. He was also an
exorcisor of spirits in later times,
as we find from a tale of the
XXth Dynasty, where we read
of his image being sent to
Bekhten to cure a possessed

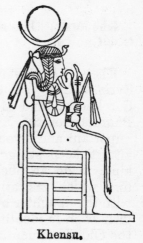

Khensu.

princess there. He is represented as tightly swathed, wearing the side lock of youth. His proper symbol, worn on the head, is the sun disk in the crescent, and he carries a staff on which are the emblems of

life ♀ stability ᛞ and dominion ⋀.

Kheper or **Kheperà**. One of the principal gods. The actual word Kheper signifies becoming or turning,

in the sense of transformation, and the god is a type of the resurrection. He is also a form of the rising sun. He is represented as a man with a beetle for a head, or with a man's head surmounted by a beetle. The beetle being his emblem, probably became a symbol of the resurrection, and may thus account for the multitudes of beetles in stones and faïence that have been found in Egypt. On tomb walls he is seen seated in the boat of the sun. In later times the scribes frequently played upon his name in the various meanings of the word.

Kheper.

Khepersh. The royal battle helmet of the Pharaohs (*See* CROWN.)

Kheta. A powerful people on the north east of Syria, whose capitals of Kadesh on the Orontes, Carchemish and Megiddo were looked upon by the Pharaohs of the XVIIIth and XIXth Dynasties as important and favourite points of attack. Ramses II., after a keen struggle with Kheta-sar, the then Kheta king, made an offensive and defensive alliance with him, which was ratified by the marriage of the Pharaoh with the daughter of the Kheta king. Some Egyptologists wish to identify these people with the Hittites of the Old Testament.

Khian, *Sc-user-en-Rā.* From the form of the

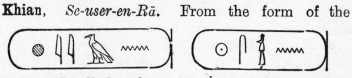

scarabs and cylinders found bearing this king's name, he may be placed with tolerable certainty in Dynasty X., cir. 3100 B.C.

Khnemu or **Khnem.** A deity wor-shipped chiefly at Philae, where he is represented as making mankind out of clay upon a potter's wheel. His name signifies the "moulder." He is represented as a ram-headed god, and is often found in conjunction with Åmen; Åmen Khnem being identified by the Greeks with their Zeus-Ammon, or Jupiter Ammon in Latin sculptures.

Khnemu.

Khu. The "luminous," the "clear." Renouf points out that "glory" is perhaps the true meaning of it. It is one of the immortal parts of man, and probably represents the spirit; it is symbolized by a flame of fire.

Khu-en-åten or **Akh-en-Åten.** *See* ÅMEN-HETEP IV.

Khufu. Second king of

Dynasty IV., cir. 3969 B.C. Reigned 63 years. The name of one daughter is known, Henut-sen. This king was the builder of the Great Pyramid of Gîzeh. There is a rock tablet at Wady Maghârah containing his cartouche.

Khut-Åten[1] (TEL EL AMARNA). The name that Amen-hetep IV., who took the name of Akh-en-Åten, gave to the new city that he built and made

---

[1] Now called Åkht-Aten.

his capital. On account of the hatred with which
his successors regarded the new form of religion he
had started, they completely destroyed the town,
temple, and palace. The few remains that have
been recovered show an enormous advance in art,
in design and adaptation. Petrie in the course of
excavations uncovered some beautiful painted pave-
ments with most charming decorative treatment.
These are evidently parts of the floor of the palace.
(*See* AMEN-ḤETEP IV.)

Kohl. *Uaz* and *Meszemt*. Green and black cosmetic
used for painting the eyelids and eyebrows in order
to make the eyes look large. Healing properties were
also ascribed to the use of it; for in the Leyden
Museum there is a toilet box with four divisions, and
the purposes of the different preparations are thus
described ; "for opening the sight," "for expelling
tears," "for expelling the flower," "daily eye-paint."
Sulphide of lead, sulphate of lead, green carbonate of
copper appear to have entered largely into the composition of kohl, which points distinctly to commercial
intercourse with the east from the earliest period of
Egyptian history. (*See* STIBIUM.)

Kummeh. A crude brick fort standing on a natural
eminence on the east bank of the Nile, about thirty
miles above the first cataract. It was built by
Usertsen III. as a protection against the Nubians.
(*See* SEMNEH.)

Kynonpolis. The Greek name for *Ka-sa ;* the capital
of the seventeenth nome of Upper Egypt, the modern
El Kes. The chief deity worshipped there was Anubis.

L

Labyrinth, *Lape-ro-hun-t.* "Temple at the opening of the canal" (Brugsch). Herodotus, ii. 148, says that it lay a little above Lake Moeris, near the city named after the crocodiles. Strabo, who visited it, states that it lay between thirty and forty stadia from the first sailing into the canal, and that Arsinoë lay about 100 stadia further on. It must therefore have been situated between Arsinoë and the entrance to the Fayûm, and not on the further side of the Birket el-Kurûn, as some have thought. Hawâra is identified by Petrie as the site of the Labyrinth.

According to Herodotus, "the pyramids may individually be compared to many of the magnificent structures of Greece, but even these are inferior to the Labyrinth. It is composed of twelve courts, all of which are covered; their entrances are opposite to each other, six to the north, and six to the south; one wall encloses the whole; the apartments are of two kinds, there are 1500 above the surface of the ground and as many beneath, in all 3000. . . . . The upper apartments I myself saw, and I pronounce them among the greatest efforts of human industry and art. The almost infinite number of winding passages through the different courts excited my warmest admiration, from spacious halls I passed through smaller apartments, and from them again to large and magnificent courts, almost without end. The ceilings and walls are all of marble, the latter richly adorned with the finest sculpture, and around each court are pillars of the whitest and most polished marble." Strabo speaks of the long and intricate passages which led to the peristyle courts, all backing on to one wall—and of the hall of twenty-seven columns, connected with the courts, the number of them being equal to the nomes of Egypt. Pliny, who appears to have strung together a number of traditional reports, says there were sixteen nome courts with forty statues of Nemesis in them. He also mentions the crocodile burying places.

Petrie, taking Herodotus and Strabo for his guides, carefully surveyed the ground in 1889, and decided that no other site than Hawâra was possible for the Labyrinth. Here he found an enormous area—1000 ft. by 800 ft.—well defined with a bed of limestone chips, and traces beneath it of a foundation, evidently prepared to receive some enormous building. " Mere figures will not signify readily to the mind the vast extent of construction ; but when we compare it with the greatest of other Egyptian temples it may be somewhat realized. On that space could be erected the great hall of Karnak and all the successive temples adjoining it, and the great court and pylons of it ; also the temple of Mut and that of Khensu, and that of Åmen-ḥetep III. at Karnak ; also the two great temples of Luxor, and still there would be room for the whole of the Ramessēum. In short all of the temples on the east of Thebes and one of the largest on the west bank, might be placed together in the one area of the ruins of Hawâra. Here we certainly have a site worthy of the renown which the Labyrinth acquired." From careful observations made on the spot, Petrie has recovered this much of the arrangement of the Labyrinth :—On the eastern side may yet be seen part of the limestone pavement, which has survived the needs of the French engineers who laid the Fayûm railway and used it as their stone quarry. This pavement appears to have been double, and consisted of blocks of yellow limestone with fine white limestone slabs superimposed. A few of the blocks of the architraves still lie about, bearing the cartouches of Åmen-em-ḥāt III. (Dynasty XII.) and Sebekneferu (Dynasty XIII.), as do also the fragments of a clustered column, and the remains of three red granite columns. From the levels it is clear that the building was square, with structures thrown out on the east side ; that "the level was uniform except along the N. edge (perhaps outside the building) and at the N.E. outbuildings; that red granite columns were used, but more likely only in the northern part of the site; and built pillars rather than monolith columns seem to belong to the part south of the cross wall." It is quite evident that, unlike Egyptian temples, which consisted of one inner shrine with chambers or courts built round it, the Labyrinth never had a central shrine, but that each court formed a little temple by itself.

Lake Moeris. The large natural basin in the Fayûm, which was transformed by the kings of Dynasty XII. into a great lake. Amen-em-ḥāt III. must have the credit of securing the lake within fixed limits, and regulating the flow of water in and out, and of damming out from it by a huge embankment a tract of land about forty square miles in area, which he drained, and which thus became one of the most fertile spots in all Egypt.

Lake Moeris, lit. *Mer-ur*, "the great lake," which at the present day is represented by the Birket el Kurûn, is about 130 feet below sea level, and it is calculated that it contains 1,500,000,000 cubic metres of water. It abounds in fish.

In the Cairo Museum there is a very interesting papyrus which represents Lake Moeris and the canal which connected it with the Nile. Round the lake basin are marked a number of towns and shrines. From this papyrus we learn that the ancient names for Lake Moeris were, *She*, "the lake," and *She ur*, "the great lake"; while the surrounding district was known by the appellation of *Ta She*, "the lake land," of which the modern Fayûm is an exact translation.

Lamentations of Isis and Nephthys. The subject of the second part of a papyrus, now No. 1425 in the Royal Berlin Museum, found by Passalaqua in the interior of a statue of Osiris.   The first part of the papyrus contains some chapters of the funeral ritual in hieroglyphs.   The second part consists of five pages of fine hieratic writing of the lower epoch, probably of the time of the Ptolemies.   The subject is the resurrection and renewed birth of Osiris, and it has a great analogy with the "Book of Respirations."   (*See* " Festival Songs of Isis and Nephthys." For translation by M. de Horrack, see "Records of the Past," 2nd edition, vol. II.)

Language. The language of the hieroglyphs is perhaps the oldest in the world.   It is closely related to no other with the exception of its descendant, Coptic (*q.v.*).   It has affinities, however, with many ; with Hebrew and other Semitic languages, with East African languages, such as Bishari, Galla, and Somali, and with the Berber languages of North Africa. During the thousands of years that it was in use it naturally came through different phases.   For practical purposes students have divided the period into three sections, called Old Egyptian, Middle Egyptian, and Late Egyptian, corresponding to the historical divisions of Old, Middle, and New Empires.   In the most ancient times it was written with purely phonetic signs, and was very little inflected.   No treatise or grammar of any kind, or of any period has been found.

Lasso. Tomb pictures at Beni Hasan show the capture of wild bulls and gazelles by means of the lasso.   The Egyptian lasso appears to have been a long rope with a ball at the end of it, which would give weight and enable the rope to catch more certainly round the legs, body or horns of the animal.

Latopolis. See Esneh.

Latus. See Fish.

Lead. This metal has been found used as inlay on doors and furniture. " Also small statuettes were occasionally made in this metal, especially those of Osiris and Anubis."

Leg, the. A constellation identified by Renouf with Cassiopeia.

Letopolis. The Greek name for *Sekhem*, the capital of the second nome of Lower Egypt, the modern Usim. Chief deity, Horus.

Library. Although no great collection of books, such as the treasure of clay tablets in Assyria, has ever been found in Egypt, there is sufficient evidence to show that collections of papyri were formed. A chamber in the temple at Edfu, off the *Khent Hall*, was a library, the catalogue of books being inscribed on its walls. The name of at least one librarian has come down to us, that of Âmen-em-hant, director of the Theban Library under Ramses II.

Libyans. Libya was the country lying north-west of Egypt, inhabited by tribes with whom the Pharaohs kept up an intermittent warfare. The Libyans of classical geographies—the *Labu, Laubu, Lebu* of the Egyptian monuments—are mentioned for the first time in the XIXth Dynasty. They are represented in paintings as rather fine men, with fair hair falling in a side lock, having fair complexions, with blue eyes. Whenever there was a conspiracy among the petty kings against Egypt, the Libyan king was, if not actual leader, at least one of the chief ringleaders. When Ramses conquered them they made splendid troops for him, and formed an important part of his auxiliary army.

Linen. The manufacture of linen was one of the most important industries. It was used for clothing, being considered purer than woollen garments, and immense quantities were used in the mummifying of men and animals. In a tomb at Medûm there is a list

of different kinds of linen.   Three are mentioned, and
of each kind there are three qualities.   Pliny mentions
four qualities, naming them after the districts from
which they came.   The finest quality almost resembles
an Indian muslin.   Examination shows that there
were always many more threads in the woof than in
the warp.   (See WEAVING and DYEING.)

Lion.   In ancient times there must have been many
lions in the desert and in Ethiopia, for there are
records of lion-hunts, with immense bags as the result.
Some historical scarabs of Åmen-ḥetep III. record
that during his reign he caught or killed a hundred
and two lions.   The animal is often seen upon temple
and tomb walls.   The king is frequently accompanied
by a favourite tame lion into battle, and the same
animal reposes under his chair at home.   It was also
apparently used in the chase, as seen on tomb walls.
The Egyptian artist was more successful in drawing
this beast than in many of his animal portraits.   In
papyri two lions seated back to back, with the solar
disk between them, is a frequent vignette.   Over one
is written " Yesterday," and over the other "This
Morning."   Shu and Tefnut are also depicted as two
lions.   The solar goddesses Sekhet, Tefnut, Pakht
and Bast are all at times represented with the lioness-
head.

Litanies of Seker.   See FESTIVAL SONGS OF ISIS
AND NEPHTHYS.

· Literature.   Numberless papyri have been found in
Egypt, the greater part of which relate to religious
matters.   This is natural, since these documents were
buried with the dead, and were then well preserved.
But on account of the perishable material on which
literature finds its expression, what is left to us must
be but a small proportion of the " books " of ancient
Egypt.   There is plenty of evidence that the art of
literature was practised at a very early time, nor is it

likely that other arts, such as that of sculpture, should have reached such perfection, and the writer's art have remained undeveloped. Of the papyri that remain the subjects are very varied. There are moral precepts (*see* PTAH-ḤETEP), hymns and love-songs, mathematical and medical treatises, judicial inquiries, religious works, one epic (*see* PENTAUR), letters, literary criticism and fiction. The drama alone is unrepresented. (*See* PAPYRI.)

ΛΟΓΙΑ ΙΗΣΟΥ (*Logia Iēsou*). A fragment of a papyrus book found at the site of the ancient Oxyrhynchus, the modern Behnesa, containing "Sayings of our Lord," and dating back in all probability to A.D. 300. Discovered and edited by Messrs. Grenfell and Hunt.

Lotus. The true Egyptian lotus is the *Nymphoea Lotus*, a white flower, of which the *Nymphoea Coerula* is the blue variety. It is quite different from the so-called rose lotus, which is really the *Nelumbium Speciosum*, and not a lotus. It was held sacred, because the Egyptians saw in it a symbol of the rising again of the sun. As such, it is found on the head of the god Nefer Tum ; and Horus is represented issuing from its cup. It was the original motive of much Egyptian decorative work, and by this means has had a far-reaching influence on ancient art. Both from the bud and full-blown forms Egyptian architects designed capitals for columns : and in ornaments, large and small, it is found in great variety. Ladies are represented with it in their hands, and it figures on altars of offerings. As an amulet it signified the divine gift of eternal youth. The most realistic representations of the plant are so conventional in form that it is difficult to distinguish between it and pictures of the papyrus plant.

Lycopolis. The Greek name for *Saud*, the capital of the thirteenth nome of Upper Egypt, the modern

Asyût.   Chief deity, Ȧp-uat.   This name, "the city
of wolves," came from the jackal-headed form of the
god worshipped there.

M

Maāt.   One of the most important goddesses of the
Egyptian Pantheon.   She is truth and justice personified; but more also, for the word *maāt* signifies
order and law, moral and physical.   Gods and kings
all confessed to "ānkh en maāt," i.e. "living or
existing by or upon rule," as if they recognized "the
unerring order which governs the universe."   She is

Maāt.

associated with Thoth, and in the
conception of these two divinities
we find probably the loftiest ideas
that the Egyptians had of the deity.
Maāt is spoken of as the daughter
of Rā.   She seems to have assisted
Ptah and Khnemu at the creation.
She is "mistress of heaven, ruler of
earth, and president of the nether
world."   Her symbol is the feather,
which we see in the judgment
scenes weighed in the balances
against the heart of the deceased.
The Greeks identified her with their
Themis.   She is represented as a woman with the
feather of truth on her head, and sometimes with
a bandage over her eyes.

Maāt Kheru ⟨symbol⟩.   A formula in inscriptions
added after the name of the deceased.   The exact
translation of it has for long been a subject of discussion among scholars.   Renouf considers that "one

whose word is law" approximates most closely to
the original; while Maspero would translate it "true
of intonation," in allusion to the true voice required
by the departed for the recitation of those magic
incantations which would render them all-powerful
in the underworld.

Mammisi. "House of giving birth." That chamber
in a temple in which the goddess is supposed to have
given birth to the third person of the triad.

Manetho. A historian of the Alexandrian school,
who, under Ptolemy Philadelphus (third century B.C.)
wrote a history of Egypt with a list of its thirty
dynasties, which he professed to have drawn from
genuine archives in the keeping of the priests. He
himself was an Egyptian priest, living at Sebennytus,
in Lower Egypt. His book is now only known by
some lists and fragments preserved by Josephus in
his treatise "Against Apion," by Eusebius in his
"Chronica," and by Syncellus. Of these, Syncellus
does not quote from the original. Though Egyptian
monuments have afforded confirmation of many of
his statements, it is not wise to rely entirely on his
assertions, since through transcriptions and retran-
scriptions the original has probably suffered from
alterations. His method was apparently not strictly
chronological, the number of years for each dynasty
being made up of the sum of the kings' reigns,
without allowance being made for the overlapping of
some of these dynasties. The work is, however,
invaluable to the student for comparative use. Several
other works have been ascribed to Manetho.

Mashuasha. The name of a tribe of Libyans, frequently occurring on the monuments, against whom
the Pharaohs waged war. They allied themselves
with other tribes against Mer-en-Ptah, and were
defeated. But again they caused trouble under
Ramses III., when they seem to have settled in the

Delta. Ramses, however, drove them out, and sub-
sequently they seem to have become auxiliaries in
that Pharaoh's army. (*See* LIBYANS.)

Mason. The "builder of walls" (Sallier Pap. II.),
a trade which is represented as being one of the
hardest and least profitable.

Mastăba. The Arabic word for the benches that
are usually placed at the entrance of Arab doorways,
and applied by the Arabs to the tombs of the Ancient
Empire found at Sakkâra, Medûm, &c. The name
was adopted by Mariette, and is recognized among
archaeologists. The mastăba consists of a quad-
rangular massive building with inclined walls, having
no opening but the door. It is low, and flat on the
top, having the appearance of a truncated pyramid.
It was built of stone or of crude brick. When of
stone the façade was decorated with sculptures. Like
every Egyptian tomb (*see* TOMBS) these ancient ones
consist of three parts—the chapel, the passage (con-

sisting in this case of a
vertical shaft), and the sarcophagus chamber. The
chapel of a mastăba takes
various forms. In some
cases it is no more than a
façade, with a false door
and a stela setting forth the
names and titles of the
deceased, the mastăba being
a solid mass of rubble. The
door is usually on the east
side, the mastăba being
roughly orientated to the
four cardinal points. In
other examples, as in the
tombs of Thi and Mera at
Sakkâra, the chapel con-
sists of a succession of

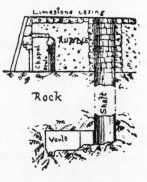

Mastăba.

chambers, some of which are dedicated to the wife or son of the deceased, the stela being placed in one of the rooms. In some, statues of the owner of the tomb have been found, either placed near the stela or put away in a *serdāb* (*q.v.*). The walls of the chambers are covered with coloured pictures, sometimes in relief and sometimes merely painted. The scenes represent the employments of the deceased during his lifetime, hunting in the desert, fishing, fowling, games, agricultural and domestic scenes. The gods are rarely mentioned. Somewhere in the floor of one of the chambers is the closed entrance to the shaft or passage leading to the sarcophagus chambers. When the mummy was deposited this shaft was filled up with rubble, upon which water was poured to make it hard.

Mathematics. The Rhind Papyrus in the British Museum gives specimens of arithmetical and geometrical problems. These are of a simple kind, but the working out is complicated, and in some cases almost impossible to follow, Egyptian mathematical knowledge being evidently very limited. The papyrus belongs to the best period of the Ramesside Dynasty. It has been translated and published by Eisenlohr and F. Ll. Griffith.

Māti. The boat of the sun in the evening. (*See* BARKS.)

Medical Papyri. The most important is the Ebers Papyrus, a work probably of the XVIIIth Dynasty, discovered by Prof. Ebers, one-fourth of which is concerned with diseases of the eye. The BERLIN MEDICAL PAPYRUS has been studied by Brugsch (*Monuments*, L. 101) and by Chabas (*Mélanges égyptol.* 1re Série). The LEYDEN PAPYRUS (Pleyte, *Études* I.); the EDWARD SMITH PAPYRUS from Thebes; and a papyrus in the BRITISH MUSEUM (Birch, *Zeitschrift*, 1871, p. 61) complete the list of those at present known.

Medicine. There is sufficient evidence of the practice of medicine among the ancient Egyptians. It seems that dissection was forbidden from religious scruples and surgical operations were prohibited, therefore the knowledge that physicians had of the organs of the body and their functions was necessarily limited. The Ebers papyrus says that the head contains twenty-two vessels, which draw the spirits (of life) into it and send them thence through the body. The heart was called " the beginning of all the members, because its vessels lead to all the members," and perhaps some idea of the circulation of the blood is indicated by the fact that the student is told that wherever the doctor laid his hand, " everywhere does he meet with the heart " (pulse). The medical papyri consist chiefly of prescriptions mixed up with magical formulæ. Against some of these recipes the practitioner has written comments as to their efficacy. The drugs were chiefly composed of vegetables, but parts of animals and insects were also used. (*See* MEDICAL PAPYRI.)

Medinet el-Fayûm. A town in the Fayûm, called anciently *Shed*, probably in reference to its being " saved," or " cut out," from the surrounding lake district. Later on it was known as Crocodilopolis, from being the centre of the crocodile worship. In Ptolemaic times it was called Arsinoë, in honour of the sister-wife of Ptolemy Philadelphus. There are ruins of a temple.

Mehit. A goddess—the personification of the north wind.

Mehurt. The name given to the great celestial heifer of whom the sun was born, and hence a personification of that part of the sky in which the sun rises and takes his daily course. She is at times identified with Nut and again with Hathor. Besides being represented as a cow, she is portrayed as a woman, sometimes with a cow's head. The judgment scene in the "Book of the Dead," was supposed to take place in the "abode of Mehurt."

Memnon. An Ethopian, son of Tithonus and Aurora, who was slain by Achilles at Troy. The two colossal statues of Åmen-ḥetep III. at Thebes were said by the Greeks to be representations of this person. These statues were originally monoliths of red breccia, a pebbly conglomerate exceedingly difficult to work. The northernmost having been severely damaged—it is supposed by the earthquake in B.C. 27—presented a curious phenomenon, emitting sounds at sunrise, which caused it to be called Vocal Memnon and brought it great fame. Many travellers came from far to hear the musical sounds, and some have left records of their experiences inscribed on the legs and pedestal of the statue. The clumsy restoration, by means of five courses of sandstone, which was effected by Septimius Sevērus, put a stop to the sounds. Among those who left inscriptions were Asklepiodotos, Balbilla a court poetess, and several governors of Egypt. The phenomenon is discussed by Strabo—who could not believe that the sound actually proceeded from the stone—by Pausanias and Juvenal. (*See* COLOSSI.)

Memnonium. Name given by the Greeks to the temple of Åmen-ḥetep III. at Thebes, with its surrounding dwellings, of which little remains but the two colossi. Also called the Amenophium. (*See* MEMNON.)

Memphis. Greek name for *Mennefert*, the capital of the first nome of Lower Egypt, the modern Mit Rahîneh. Chief deity, Ptah.

Menà. 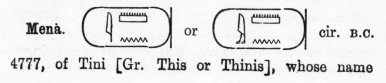 or cir. B.C. 4777, of Tini [Gr. This or Thinis], whose name

signifies "the Steadfast," was the first king of the
Ist Dynasty. All that is known of him consists
of a few statements of doubtful credit found
in the classic writers, there being no monuments
left of the period. These tell us that he united
Egypt under one sceptre and was its first law-
giver ; that he founded Memphis, and that, in order
to secure a suitable site for his capital, he diverted the
course of the Nile by the construction of an enormous
dike. The French engineer, M. Linant, professes to
have found this construction in the great dike of
Cocheiche. Tradition says that he was followed by
his seven sons in succession.

Mendes. The Greek name for *Pa-ba-néb-tettet*, capital of the sixteenth nome of Lower Egypt, the modern
El-Amdid. Chief deity, Ba-neb-Tettet.

Menḥit. A lion-headed goddess akin to Hathor and
Bast, representing some form or degree of the heat of
the sun. She was worshipped at Heliopolis.

Men-ka-Rā, *Nit-aqerti.* Probably the Queen

Nitocris of Manetho and Herodotus. She was the last
ruler of the VIth Dynasty, cir. 3347 B.C.

Men-kau-Hor. The

seventh king of the Vth Dynasty, cir. 3589 B.C.
There is a rock tablet of this king at Wady Maghârah.

Men-kau-Rā. Fourth

king of the IVth Dynasty, cir. B.C. 3845. Reigned
sixty-three years. The builder of the third of the

great pyramids at Gîzeh. The lid of the wooden coffin bearing the king's name, and a skeleton supposed to be his are in the British Museum.

Mentu. The Egyptian war god. He was one of the solar gods adored at Thebes; his cult there was at one time as important as that of Ámen. It is probable that he was the original god of the district between Kus and Gebelên, Ámen being a later form. The chief centre of it was at Hermonthis (Erment). His wife at that place was Rā-t-taui. The bull was sacred to him, being in this case called *Bakh*, an equivalent to the Mnevis-bull of Rā. Mentu is represented as a hawk-headed man wearing a solar disk and two plumes. Ramses II. in the wrath of battle compares himself to his "father Mentu."

Mentu.

Mentu-ḥetep I.,

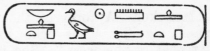

Neb-ḥetep. Second king of Dynasty XI., cir. 2965 B.C.

Mentu-ḥetep II. *Neb-taui-Rā.* Fifth king of Dy-

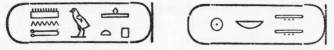

nasty XI., cir. 2922 B.C., and son of Queen Am. Inscriptions bearing this king's name are found in the quarries of Hammamât. A tablet at Konosso states that he conquered thirteen tribes.

Mentu-ḥetep III., *Neb-kher-Rā.* Eighth king of

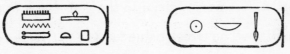

Dynasty XI., cir. 2832 B.C. Two queens are known,
Tumem (?) and Åāḥ.

Mer-en-Ptah, 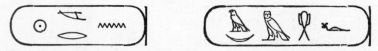 Dynasty XIX,

cir. B.C. 1300. The 14th son of Ramses II. It is
generally believed that this king may be identified
with the Pharaoh of the Exodus. His body was
discovered in the tomb of Åmen-ḥetep II. in 1899;
and is now in the Cairo Museum. An irruption of
the Libyans into Egypt and their defeat at Prosopis is
the chief event of this otherwise uneventful reign.

Mer-en-Rā, *Meḥti-em-sa-f.* Fourth king of Dynasty

VI., cir. 3447 B.C. The important inscription in the
tomb of Her-khuf at Aswân dates from this king's
reign. His pyramid, *Men ānkh,* is at Sakkâra.

Mer-sker. A form of the goddess Hathor. Her
name signifies " she who loves silence." She is
" regent of the west." She is represented with the
disk and horns of Hathor, and is sometimes pictured
in the " mountain of the west."

Meskhent. The goddess of birth seen on her throne
presiding over the birth scene on the walls at Dêr el
Baḥri. She also figures in the scene of the weighing
of the heart in the Judgment Hall of Osiris. The
symbol on her head is a straight stem split at the end
and curling over on either side, like the sign on the
head of Ānit (*q.v.*).

Meszemt. *See* STIBIUM and KOHL.

Mesthà. A name given to the god *Åmset* (*q.v.*).

Metēlis. The Greek name for *Sent-nefert,* the capital

of the seventh nome of Lower Egypt. Chief deity, Hu.

Min. *See* ÅMSU.

Mizraim. The Hebrew name of Egypt. It means literally the two *mazors* or towers.

Mnevis. Name of the sacred black bull venerated at Heliopolis. (*See* APIS.)

Moeris. *See* LAKE MOERIS.

Money. In the sense of coin the ancient Egyptians had no money. The first appearance of a coinage was during the Persian occupation; but no real currency was established until the Ptolemaic times. Gold for purchase-money was weighed. Under the New Empire it was made in the form of rings, but even then was weighed. The rings seem to have varied in thickness, though having a uniform diameter of about 5 ins. Such a weighing out is frequently depicted on the tomb and temple walls. "Mr. Poole's researches into the very complicated numismatics of the Ptolemaic Dynasty show that the first Ptolemy established a silver coinage on the basis of the Attic drachma as the ordinary silver unit." There was both silver and copper coinage. (*See* UTEN and TRADE.)

Monogamy. *See* HAREM.

Moon. The moon was sacred under different forms, Åāḥ, Thoth, Khensu being the most frequent. But especially is it connected with Thoth as "the

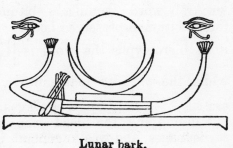

Lunar bark.

measurer," the moon being the measurer of time, and Thoth being god of all the exact sciences. In later times Osiris is identified with the moon. As a symbol it is represented as a crescent holding a disk, in which form it may be seen on the heads of Thoth, Khensu, and others. Like the sun and all the planets, the moon was conceived of as sailing the celestial ocean in his own particular bark.

Mummied Animals. Certain animals that were either emblems of, or sacred to, gods were carefully mummified by the Egyptians. Those oftenest met with are the bull, antelope, jackal, hippopotamus, cat, monkey or ape, crocodile, ichneumon, hedgehog, shrewmouse, ibis, hawk, frog, toad, scorpion, beetle, snake; and the latus, oxyrhynchus, and silurus fishes. Of these, the Apis bulls (*q.v.*) were buried in sarcophagi, many of which have been discovered at Sakkâra. Other animals were placed in rectangular bronze or wooden cases, each surmounted by a little figure of the animal it contained; or in cases which took the shape of the animals themselves. Thus cat-coffins were cat-shaped, with eyes of obsidian, rock crystal, or coloured paste. Large numbers of mummied cats have been found at Bubastis, the city where the cat-headed goddess was worshipped.

Ibises were placed in earthenware jars, while snakes and fish were often merely bandaged and laid in pits prepared for the purpose.

Mummy (human). A term probably derived from an Arab word " mumia "—bitumen, meaning, therefore, a bitumen-preserved body.

In hieroglyphs the word is ⃒ ⎯◻ ⧻ 𓅱 ♀ *Sāhu*,

while the verb to make into a mummy is ◿ ⫤

qes, lit., " to wrap up in bandages."

Mummifying the dead was practised from the earliest ages, and was in general use until the fourth

century A.D. It had for its object the preservation of
the body in order that the soul might one day return
to it and revivify it. (*See* KHAT and SĀHU.)

Music. No system of notation has come down to
us. But there are many evidences that music was
much thought of. According to Plato the rules about
music were most rigid, only certain kinds being
allowed by government. Strabo confirms this, saying
that "the children of the Egyptians were taught
letters, the songs appointed by law, and a certain
kind of music established by government, to the
exclusion of every other." Diodorus does not agree
with this, but admits that the Greek poets and
musicians visited Egypt in order to improve their
art. The origin of music was ascribed to divinity,
sometimes to Isis, but more particularly to Thoth
(*q.v.*). Primitive music consists chiefly of instruments
of percussion, followed, as culture progresses, by reeds
and flutes. But in quite early times the Egyptians
used stringed instruments of different kinds. In
Theban tombs great harps six feet high with many
strings are depicted, which indicates an advanced
knowledge of intervals. A well-known picture represents a comic procession of a donkey, a lion, a
crocodile, and an ape, playing a harp, two other
stringed instruments, and the double pipes.

Musical Instruments. Our knowledge of these is
derived from the pictures on the monuments, and
various specimens which have been found. Of
Instruments of Percussion there were two or three
kinds of drums, cymbals, a form of castanets, the
tambourine, and the sistrum (*q.v.*). The commonest
form of DRUM is a long narrow cylinder of wood or
copper, with parchment at both ends, and covered
with bracing cords. It was slung over the shoulders
and carried on the back while marching. It figures
chiefly in military scenes. A drum similar to the
modern *darabooka* is very occasionally represented on

the tomb walls. It resembles a funnel-shaped vase
of pottery with parchment strained over the wide
mouth. The CYMBALS were similar to modern ones,
only smaller. They were made of brass or a mixture
of brass and silver. The CASTANETS were in the form
of slightly curved sticks of wood or ivory about a foot
long, terminating in a human head. The pictures of
TAMBOURINES on the tomb walls do not indicate the
metal rings which we associate with the instrument.
But from the way in which the performer is seen to
hold it up we may conclude that the Egyptian tambourine was provided with them.

Of *Wind Instruments* only wooden ones have been
preserved; but pictures on the monuments show
troops accompanied by men with TRUMPETS. The
instrument represented is a simple one about $1\frac{1}{2}$ ft.
long, made apparently of brass. The FLUTE was of
various kinds. Sometimes it was of extraordinary
length—between 4 and 5 ft. The specimens found
vary from 7 to 15 ins. in length. They were made of
reeds chiefly, and had three, four, and sometimes five
holes. Flutes were also made of wood, of ivory, of
horn, and bone. The DOUBLE PIPE is more frequently
depicted on the monuments than the flute, oftenest
played by women, and sometimes while the performer
dances. It was made of the same materials as the
flute.

The *Stringed Instruments* represented on the monuments are of several kinds. Besides the HARP (*q.v.*)
there were lyres, guitars or lutes, and others of
which we do not know the names. The lyre is of
various forms, and is decorated in many ways. It
had from five to eighteen strings, which were sounded
by the hand or with a plectrum; and sometimes the
chords were touched with the left hand while the right
hand played with a plectrum. The instrument was held
in various ways, occasionally under the arm. The
GUITAR, or lute, is perhaps the instrument most frequently met with. It was played chiefly by women.
The oval body is of wood, or of wood covered with

leather perforated with several holes. With its long neck it must have measured about 4 ft. The three strings were fastened to the body by a triangular piece of wood or bone, and kept from contact with the neck at the other end by a small cross bar.

Musicians. There must have been two kinds of music, and their exponents belonged to very different grades in society. The higher kind, which was probably very stereotyped, was taught and performed by the priests, and was more or less religious, while the popular music which the people loved to have at their feasts was provided by paid entertainers who were usually accompanied by dancers, if indeed they did not dance themselves. That the Pharaoh enjoyed singing and musical entertainments is evident from the fact that there was a functionary who bore the title " Superintendent of song and of the recreation of the king"; but the king never seems to have done particular honour to any performers, nor do we hear of any musician of high rank. There were both men and women performers. (*See* MUSIC and MUSICAL INSTRUMENTS.)

Mut. A goddess, the second of the Theban triad, where she is the wife of Amen-Rā and the mother of Khensu. Her name signifies "the mother," the vulture which stands for it also meaning "mother." She is called "mistress of the gods, lady of heaven, eye of Rā." Amen-hetep III. built a temple to her in Asher, the chief centre of her worship, which is a little south of Karnak. She is represented as a woman wearing the vulture cap and the double crown. Sometimes she is figured with a lioness' head.

Mut.

Mut-em-ua. Co-heiress, with her sister Khut, of Åmen-ḥetep II., wife of Thothmes IV. and mother of Åmen-ḥetep III. She is represented standing to the left of the king her son in the Colossi at Thebes, and on the walls of the temple of Luxor.

Mythology. *See* RELIGION.

N

Natron, i.e. neutral carbonate of sodium, obtained from the natron lakes which are in a valley in the desert west of the Delta, not very far from the river. This substance, used in the preparation of the body for entombment (*see* EMBALMING) was probably obtained by evaporation of the water of the lakes; or by washing the efflorescence from the earth on which it appeared.

Nahar, or **Nahal.** A Semitic word signifying "river"; and by Brugsch it is thought to be the origin of the word "Nile."

Naukratis. A town in the north-west of the Delta, in the fifth nome of Lower Egypt, not far from Saïs, about $6\frac{1}{2}$ miles due north of the modern Kom el Hism. Strabo says it was founded by Milesians in the fifth century B.C., but this must be an error, because in the sixth century B.C. Amāsis granted privileges to it. Herodotus, speaking of Amāsis' favour to the Greeks, says that he gave the city of Naukratis for such as arrived in Egypt to dwell in. During his reign it enjoyed a monopoly of Greek trade and flourished.

Its prosperity declined under the Persian invasion, but revived under Alexander. It suffered, however, by the growth of its new rival, Alexandria, and was probably extinct as a city about the beginning of the third century. During its period of prosperity it had attained a position of literary as well as commercial eminence.

The site has been excavated by Petrie, who discovered remains of the archaic temples of Apollo and Aphrodite, of which Herodotus and Athenaios speak.

Neb-taui, i.e. *"lord of the two lands,"* usually thought to mean ruler of Upper and Lower Egypt. It is more likely, however, that the two lands represent the country east and west of the Nile.

Nectanebo II., *Kheper-ka-Rā*, B.C. 361-340, XXXth

Dynasty. The last native king of Egypt, who was defeated by Darius Ochus, the Persian, at Pelusium. Instead of defending his kingdom, Nectanebo shut himself up in Memphis and devoted himself to magic. He eventually fled to Napata, in Nubia.

Needle. *See* OBELISK.

Needles. Bronze needles have been found measuring about 8-10 centimetres. But they are large, and only suitable for coarse work.

Nefer-ka-Rā, *Ḥeni*. Ninth king of IIIrd Dynasty. Reigned twenty-six (?) years. It is thought that the Ḥeni mentioned in the Prisse Papyrus as the predecessor of Sneferu, the first king of the Vth Dynasty, may be identified with this king.

Nefert-ári, or **Áāḥmes-Nefert-ári**,

was the sister and wife of Áāḥmes I. of the XVIIIth

Dynasty, and was really the foundress of that line, and as such she was adored until the XXIst Dynasty. Her beautiful coffin, 10 ft. 4 ins. long, is in the Cairo Museum.

Nefer Tum, or **Nefer-àtmu**. The third god in the triad of Memphis, the others being Ptah and Sekhet, though his place is frequently taken by Imhetep. He was the son of Sekhet, or Pakht, or Bast. As a nature god he represents the heat of the rising sun. In the "Book of the Dead" his function seems to be to grant continuance of life in the world to come, but he is not very frequently mentioned. He is represented as a man with a lotus springing from his head. Miniature figures of this god in various substances are comparatively common.

Nehesi. A king, probably to be placed among those of the XIIIth Dynasty. His name suggests that he may have been a negro.

Nefer Tum.

Nehesiu. The Egyptian name for the negroes.

Neit, or **Neith**, or **Nit**. A goddess whose name is found in the oldest inscriptions, although her cult does not seem to have gained much prominence until the time of the XXVIth Dynasty, and then it was confined to Saïs. There she formed a triad with Osiris and Horus. She is represented as a woman wearing the crown of Lower Egypt, and her distinguishing emblems are sometimes the shuttle and sometimes two crossed arrows. She frequently carries a bow and arrows in her hands, and in this

Neit.

form has been identified by the Greeks with their
Athene (Minerva). She may have been of Libyan
origin, for we see her symbol, the shuttle, much used
as a decorative design by that nation. Her name
signifies the "weaver" or the "shooter." At times
she is identified with the sky goddess, and is represented
as a cow. At other times she assumes the attributes
of Mut, or Hathor. She is said to be the "mother of
the gods," particularly of Rā, and—in a pyramid text
—of Sebek.

Nekau II., *Nem-àb-Rā*, XXVIth Dynasty, B.C. 612-

596. The Pharaoh Necho of the Old Testament
(2 Kings xxiii. 29, Jeremiah xlvi. 2), a brave and ener-
getic ruler, but wanting in prudence. He maintained
a fleet at the mouths of the Nile and on the Red Sea,
and with the aid of Phoenician sailors, circumnavigated
Africa. He also attempted to re-cut the canal from
Bubastis to the head
of the Gulf of Suez.

Nekhebt (*Sivan*).
The goddess of the
South. She is usually
represented in the

Nekhebt.

form of a vulture. She was worshipped at Eileithyias.

Nephthys. Sister goddess to Isis,
and wife of Set. She helped Isis in
her search for the body of the slain
Osiris, and in her lamentations over
him. Therefore she is always associated with Isis in funerary scenes.
The two stand facing each other with
wings outspread on either side of the
mummy, or they are carved at each
Nephthys.   end of sarcophagi, or painted on

coffins and mummies. Nephthys, or Nebt-het, is the daughter of Seb and Nut, and as a nature goddess represents, probably, the sunset. She is depicted as a woman, her only distinguishing feature being her head-dress. According to Plutarch's legend, she was the mother of Anubis.

Nesi-Âmsu, papyrus of, found at Thebes in 1860; purchased by Rhind and sold to the trustees of the British Museum by David Bremner. Owing to the careless writing of the colophon, it has been concluded that the papyrus was not written specially for Nesi-Âmsu, but was one of a number prepared by some person whose business it was to supply funeral papyri to relatives of the dead, for placing in the tombs. It consists of three separate works : first, the Festival Songs of Isis and Nephthys (*q.v.*) ; secondly, the Litanies of Seker (*q.v.*) ; and thirdly, the Book of the Overthrowing of Âpepi (*q.v.*). The whole papyrus, which is of very fine texture, and measures 19 ft. by $9\frac{1}{2}$ ins. (containing 33 columns and 940 lines), has been transliterated and translated by Budge in Archaeologia, vol. 52, part ii.

Neter-khertet. A name for the " divine under-world," which frequently occurs in the " Book of the Dead " and in tomb inscriptions.

Neter-ta. " The Divine land " ; probably the country along the Red Sea extending from Suez on the north to the mountains on the south.

Nif. ⟗ The little sail was the symbol for breath. The *ba* (*q.v.*) may be seen bringing it back to the mummy.

Nile. ὁ Νεῖλος, Nilus, Nîl, the name of the river of Egypt. It is almost unnecessary to remark that these names are none of them ancient Egyptian. The derivation of the word " Nile " is given by Brugsch as coming from the Semitic "Nahar" or "Nahal," signifying a "river." The hieroglyphic names for the river of Egypt are—

(1) 𓎛𓊪𓇋𓈗 *Hāpi*, "he who overspreadeth," an undoubted reference to the inundation.

(2) 𓏇𓏤𓈗 *Nu*, a name it has in common with the sky, signifying "lifted up." It is an obvious allusion to the fact so often spoken of in the texts that the Nile was "raised up" from its source by a divinity who is sometimes called Isis, sometimes Sothis, and at others Hathor.

(3) 𓅠𓏤 *Uḳa*, a word expressing "rushing forth," "leaping"; another allusion to the inundation.

(4) 𓅠𓏤𓆉 *Akbà urà*, lit. "the great weeping," a recognized name for the overflowing of the Nile. The Egyptians also spoke of their river as a serpent, and even represented it thus in art. At Philae is a well-known picture which shows the Nile issuing from a cavern in the shape of a serpent. Renouf has shown that in every one of the nomes a divine serpent was worshipped, this being none other than the good genius or portion of the river which passed through that district.

The Nile is also called *Kam-urà*, the "great extender," in the "Book of the Dead," chap. 64.

This river is represented in the sculptures in human form, partaking both of the male and female sex. A group of aquatic plants forms the head-dress. It is often figured on the sides of the thrones of colossal statues, where two figures, representing the Nile of the north and the south, are seen standing opposite to each other, and binding flowers of papyrus and lotus to the *sam*. (*See* AMULETS and HÁPI.)

Statues of the Nile are very rare, and are usually painted green or red to represent the colour of the river before or after the inundation.

The source of the Nile has been from time immemorial a mystery; modern travellers place it in the Victoria Nyanza Lake, but it is quite possible that it rises even further south of the equator. The river, after passing through Lake Albert Nyanza, proceeds as far north as Gondokoro, 5° N., where it is joined by the Bahr-el-Gazelle and the Sobât; from this point to Khartûm it is called the Bahr-el-Abyad (White Nile); here the Bahr-el-Azrek (Blue Nile) unites with it. The stream then flows on to the sea, receiving on

its way only one tributary, the Atbara. Its length is about 3300 miles.

Every year the Nile overflows its banks. About the time of the summer solstice it begins gradually to rise, and continues so to do until the end of September, when it gradually subsides, leaving behind it a deposit of rich, black mud. The prosperity of the country depends upon the height to which the flood Nile rises. Should there be an excessive overflow the dikes break down, houses are swept away, and sometimes whole villages damaged. If there is a deficiency, the land

which is left unmoistened is not fertilized and must
remain barren.

As long ago as the days of Amen-em-hât III.
(Dynasty XII.) so much importance was attached to
the rising of the Nile that messengers were despatched
from Semneh, above the second cataract, to carry the
news through the towns and villages.   There are
some inscribed rocks at Semneh recording the average
height of the inundation during the reign of this
monarch, and it surpasses that of our days by 11½ ft.,
while the *highest* rise recorded is 27 ft. 3 ins. above
the greatest inundation known in our times.

Nitocris.   *See* MEN-KA-RĀ.

Nomarch.   *See* NOMES.

Nomes.   ⧕ ▭ ▦ *Ḥesep.* The great divisions of
the kingdom of ancient Egypt, and dating back to the
IVth Dynasty, where some are mentioned by name
with their chief towns.   There were in all forty-two
nomes, twenty-two in Upper Egypt, and twenty in
Lower ; each was placed under the protection of one
particular divinity ; and each had two capitals, one
civil, the other religious, the former being the seat of
government.   The office of governor was hereditary,
passing from the father to the eldest grandson on the
mother's side (Brugsch).   There were four divisions
of the nome :—

(*a*) *Nut*, the chief town.

(*b*) The cultivated land.

(*c*) The marsh land, which, under certain conditions, could be cultivated.

(*d*) The canals, sluices, &c.

The following is a list with the names of the
modern towns or villages that most nearly mark their
sites :—

NOMES OF UPPER EGYPT.

I.	Ta-Kens	Aswân.
II.	Tes-Hor	Edfu.
III.	Ten	Esneh.
IV.	Uast	Karnak.
V.	Herui	Kuft.
VI.	Äati	Dendera.
VII.	Sekhem	Hou.
VIII.	Äbt	Girgeh.
IX.	Ämsu	Akhmîm.
X.	Uazet	Itfu.
XI.	Set	Shodb.
XII.	Tu-f	Kau el Kebîr.
XIII.	Atef-khent	Asyût.
XIV.	Atef-peh	Kusîya.
XV.	Un	Eshmunên.
XVI.	Meh-mahet	Minieh.
XVII.	Änup	El-Kes.
XVIII.	Sep	El-Hibeh.
XIX.	Uab	Behneseh.
XX.	Am-Khent	Ahnasieh.
XXI.	Am-peh	Ashment.
XXII.	Maten	Atfîh.

NOMES OF LOWER EGYPT.

I.	Aneb-hez	Bedrashên.
II.	Aā	Usîm.
III.	Äment	Kom el Hism.
IV.	Sepi-res	
V.	Sepi-meht	Sa el Hagar.
VI.	Ka-set	Sakha.
VII.	Nefer-äment	
VIII.	Nefer-äbt	Tel el Maskhuta.
IX.	Azi	Abusîr.
X.	Ka-kam	Benha el-Asal.
XI.	Ka-hebes	Horbeit.
XII.	Teb-neter	Samanhûd.
XIII.	Hek-at	Ain esh-Shams.
XIV.	Khent-äbt	Sân.

Nomes of Lower Egypt (*Continued*).

XV.	Tehuti	.	.	.	El-Bakalîyeh.
XVI.	Khar	.	.	.	El-Amdîd.
XVII.	Sam-hut	.	.	.	Ebshan.
XVIII.	Am-khent	.	.	.	Tell Basta.
XIX.	Am-peh	.	.	.	Nebesheh.
XX.	Sept	.	.	.	Saft el-Heneh.

The number of nomes was not always the same. The governor of a nome was called by the Greeks a nomarch. On the temple walls the nomes are represented as figures of the Nile god bringing various offerings. Such lists may be seen at Philae, Karnak, Dendera, Edfu, Abydos, &c.

Nu. The celestial ocean, the father of the gods, the water traversed by the solar bark ; perhaps the Egyptian idea of the macrocosm, since they considered him the source of all that is. Pictures of him in the "Book of the Dead" show a seated figure wearing the disk and plumes ⚕. The goddess Nut is considered to be the female manifestation of Nu.

Nu, The. The instrument used for the mystical opening of the mouth of the mummy.

Numeration. The Egyptians employed a decimal system. Units were figured thus, $|$; tens, $\cap$; hundreds, ℮ ; thousands, $\mathbinline{}$. Therefore ₹℮℮℮||| ∩∩∩ || signifies 1335.

Nut. The female principle of Nu. She is represented arching her body over the earth, which she touches with her toes and fingers. Her body is studded with stars, since she represents the sky. Frequently Shu stands underneath to support her, and Seb, the earth god, lies on the ground beneath. She is also depicted in the form of a cow. There are two

variations of the story of Nut.   One speaks of Shu
as violently separating Nut from her husband Seb.
The other tells that her father, Rā, was anxious to
leave the earth where men rebelled against his rule,

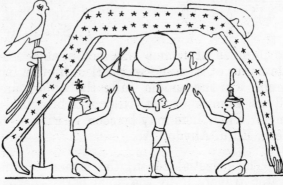

Nut.

and that Nut of her own will left Seb, and raised herself from the earth in the form of a cow, while Shu,
her son, dutifully supported her in this position.   Still
as a cow she represents the sky, in which Rā, the
sun, was safe from his troublesome mortals.

Nut.   A goddess distinct from Nut, the female principle of Nu.   She is depicted in the " Book of the
Dead " with a snake's head surmounted by a disk, or
with a cat's head.   In tombs and on stelae she is
seen emerging from a sycomore tree, and offering the
bread and water of the underworld to the deceased.
In this capacity she is sometimes confused with
Hathor (*q.v.*).

O

Oases. Owing probably to their inaccessibility, the oases in early times were regarded with a certain amount of superstition. The GREAT OASIS had been considered a kind of paradise where the dead went in search of happiness, from which fact, in all probability, came its name, " Isles of the Blessed," found in Herodotus. It was colonized in early times, as were several other oases, but there are more Ptolemaic, Roman and Coptic than Egyptian remains in these desert islands. It was to the oasis of Jupiter Ammon —modern Sîwa—that Alexander the Great went to consult the famous oracle.

Obelisk. A long square tapering shaft, with slightly convex faces, and pyramidion at the top. Obelisks were made of varying sizes and in different materials. The finest are in granite from the Aswân quarries. The largest and best worked of those still standing is that erected by Queen Hatshepsut at Karnak. It is 109 feet high, and an inscription tells how it was quarried, transported, carved, and set up in position in seven months. The obelisk at Heliopolis, which is the oldest, is 68 feet high, those at Karnak measure 77 feet and 75½ feet. Usually they were capped with bronze or gilt copper. They were placed in front of the colossi that were put on either side of the main entrance to a temple. There were always two of them, though in point of height they might not be a pair. Although many have thought that the obelisk represents some religious emblem—a finger of God, or ray of the sun—it is more probable that the idea in the minds of those who raised them was similar to that of the raisers of menhirs or standing stones. Under the IVth Dynasty we find small obelisks in the tombs placed on either side of the stela. At Begig, in the Fayûm, there is an obelisk of rectangular form, having a rounded top with a groove intended to receive some object, possibly a hawk emblem. The pyramidion of an obelisk was decorated with scenes of offerings. The sides bore perpendicular lines of hieroglyphs containing the king's names and titles, and his praises. The pedestal on which the obelisk stood was decorated with inscriptions or figures of cynocephali (*q.v.*).

Ogdoad. A cycle of eight gods and goddesses, a number not frequently met with. The example is found in the eight gods at Hermopolis, from which the town got its Egyptian name, "the city of the eight." They were four gods and their wives, and the eight seem to have been subordinate to Thoth, and figured as eight cynocephali—his sacred animal.

On. *See* HELIOPOLIS.

Osirian. A term applied to the blessed dead. As Osiris died and came to life again, so they hoped to live again ; and in that faith the epithet Osirian was applied by the Egyptians to their dead. "The Osirian" M. or N. is the formula invariably used in funerary inscriptions.

Osiris.

Osiris. *Áusàr.* "Highest of all the Powers," and the divine king of Egypt, who civilized mankind, taught them agriculture, gave them laws, and instructed them in religion. He was the son of Seb and Nut, the offspring of heaven and earth and the husband and brother of Isis. He was treacherously murdered by his brother Set—the power of darkness and evil —and his death was avenged by his son, the young Horus, who is called "the avenger of his father." After his death and resurrection, Osiris became lord of the underworld and judge of the dead; which fact accounts for the immense number of prayers that are addressed to him. As the whole hope of immortality among the Egyptians was bound up in Osiris, so in order to be as closely allied with him as possible they called their deceased by the title of "the Osirian" M. or N. Among nature gods, Osiris represents the sun, who is overcome by the night, and rises again the next morning.

The mythical legend of Osiris is told by Plutarch in "De Iside et Osiride," XII.-XX., wherein it is set forth that after his murder by Set, Isis endeavoured to recover the body, which she found washed up by the sea at Byblos. For greater safety she removed it, which Set discovering, tore open the coffin, and divided the body into fourteen parts, which he scattered throughout Egypt. For these Isis searched, and wherever she found a piece she erected a temple over the spot. This accounts for the numerous localities which claim to be the burying-place of Osiris.

Osorkon. Three kings of the XXIInd Dynasty bore this name. Monuments bearing their names are to be found not infrequently, but of their definite history but little is at present known.

Ostraca. The name given to the numerous fragments of pottery having Egyptian, Coptic, or Greek texts traced on them. Even fragments of stone have been used in this way, an evidence of the scarceness or costliness of papyrus. The writing usually consists of rough drafts made by scribes.

Ostrich. The bird was well known in ancient times, and highly prized for its plumes and its eggs. The former were used in some of the royal head-dresses and as decorations for the royal chariot horses. The eggs sometimes form part of royal tribute. The ostrich is represented on tomb walls at Thebes.

Oxyrhynchus. The Greek name for *Pa-māzet*, the capital of the nineteenth nome of Upper Egypt, the modern Behneseh. Chief deity, Set. In the fifth century it was a stronghold of Christianity. Many papyri have been found on the site.

P

Pakht.

Pakht or Pasht. A lioness - headed goddess of the same nature as Sekhet, and by some con sidered identical with her. She is a solar goddess, and represents some varia- tion of the sun heat. Her name signifies to "rend in pieces." She figures largely in the Speos Ar- temidos at Beni Hasan, the centre of her cult having been there.

Palette. The palette figured in pictures on tomb walls exactly cor- responds with those which have been found.

These consist of a rectangular block of wood varying from 10 ins. by 2 ins. to 16 ins. by $2\frac{1}{2}$ ins. and about $\frac{3}{8}$ of an inch thick. At one end are small hollows, usually only two, to hold the different pigments. Down the centre is cut a groove ending in a kind of pocket for holding the reed pens or brushes. Several palettes in other materials have been found, such as limestone, basalt, ivory, and sometimes they are inlaid or otherwise finely decorated. These, however, were probably funerary objects not intended for use. Sometimes they have been found buried with scribes, and the name of the owner is frequently engraved on them, followed by an inscription dedicating the palette to Thoth. The 94th chapter of the "Book of the Dead" contains a prayer to Thoth for a palette and ink pot.

Panopolis. Greek name for *Ápu*, capital of the ninth nome of Upper Egypt, the modern Akhmîm. Chief deity, Ámsu.

Papyri. A papyrus roll consists of several pieces of papyrus from 6 ins. to 17 ins. wide joined together to form a long sheet, which, being written on, was rolled up usually from left to right. The longest known is the Harris Papyrus in the British Museum, which measures 135 ft. in length. Being rolled up, it was tied with a piece of papyrus string and sealed with a lump of clay. One of the most familiar hieroglyphic signs is ⌒ representing the papyrus roll. The writing reads from right to left in most cases, though occasionally the signs are placed in columns. The latter applies to papyri written in linear hieroglyphs, such as the papyrus of Ani in the British Museum. The great numbers of papyri found in museums all over Europe and in private collections cover a long period of Egyptian history, and show a great diversity of style both in language and caligraphy. The earlier ones are in linear hieroglyphs and hieratic (*q.v.*), the later in demotic and Greek. The papyri of the "Book of the Dead " (*q.v.*), which form a large number of the known papyri, are frequently elaborately illustrated, in some cases with coloured pictures. These are found buried with the mummies, sometimes under the bandages, at others between the hands, on the chest, or under the arms or legs. They were also placed in wooden statues of gods hollowed out for the purpose. When found they are extremely dry and brittle, and require immense care in handling. The scribes wrote with a reed pen, using an ink which to this day retains its splendid black. Pliny says it was composed of smoke black, or the calcined dregs of wine added to gum.

There can be little doubt that the making of papyri was a kind of trade, and since no burial was considered complete without a copy of at least some chapters of the " Book of the Dead," it must have been a lucrative one. Examination shows that some of these papyri were not specially prepared for the deceased with whom they were buried, as the name has been filled in last. The following is a list of some of the best known papyri, many of which are called by the names of their finders or possessors :—

ABBOT PAPYRUS in the British Museum. *Subject,* a judicial inquiry at Thebes.

AMHERST PAPYRI, formerly in the possession of the late Lord Amherst of Hackney. *Subjects,* judicial inquiry at Thebes, tale of Sekhti and Hemti, tale of Sanehat. *Translations* by Mr. Newberry and F. Ll. Griffith.

ANASTASI PAPYRI in the British Museum. *Subject* (of longest), journey of an Egyptian officer to Syria and Palestine. *Date* about 1400 B.C. *Translation* by Chabas.

BERLIN PAPYRI. No. 1. Tale of Sanehat. *Date,* Middle Empire. *Translations* by Chabas, Goodwin, Maspero. Nos. 2 and 4 contain the Tale of Sekhti and Hemti.

EBERS PAPYRUS. Medical papyrus. *Translations* by George Ebers and Ludwig Stern.

HARRIS PAPYRUS in the British Museum. *Subjects,*

judicial inquiries, list of offerings, a discourse of Ramses III. to his chiefs. *Date* about 1225 B.C. *Translations* by Piehl, Chabas, Eisenlohr.

HARRIS PAPYRUS in the British Museum. *Subject* Magic. *Translation* by Chabas.

LEE PAPYRUS. *Subject*, Harem conspiracy.

MEDICAL PAPYRUS of Berlin. *Date*, XIXth Dynasty. *Translations* by Brugsch and Chabas.

D'ORBINEY PAPYRUS in the British Museum. *Subject*, The Romance of the Two Brothers. *Date*, XIXth Dynasty. *Translations* by Maspero, Groff, and Renouf.

PRISSE PAPYRUS in the Bibliothèque Nationale. *Subject*, Moral treatise. *Date*, Middle Empire. *Translations* by Chabas, Heath, and Virey. Called "The oldest book in the world."

RHIND PAPYRUS in the British Museum. *Subject*, Mathematics. *Date*, Ramesside period. *Translation* by Eisenlohr and Griffith.

SALLIER PAPYRI in the British Museum. No. 1. *Subject*, "History of the uprising of the Egyptians against the yoke of the foreigners," i.e. the Hyksos. *Date*, XIXth Dynasty. *Translations* by Goodwin, Chabas, Ebers, and Maspero. No. 2. *Subject*, Instructions of Àmen-em-hāt I. to his son Usertsen I. and a Hymn to the Nile. *Translations* by Maspero, Schack, and Amélineau. No. 3. *Subject*, Epic poem of Pentaur (*q.v.*). *Translations* by de Rougé, Goodwin, and Brugsch.

SETNA, PAPYRUS OF. A demotic papyrus in the Cairo Museum. *Subject*, Tale of a search for a magical book. *Date*, Ptolemaic. *Translations* by Brugsch, Revillout, Maspero, and Hess.

SHIPWRECKED SAILOR, TALE OF A. A papyrus in the Hermitage collection at St. Petersburg. *Date*, XIIth or XIIIth Dynasty. *Translations* by Goleni-scheff and Maspero.

TURIN PAPYRI. The most famous of these is the list of kings, which is so important to chronologers.

Professor Maspero has published several old Egyptian tales under the title of "Contes Populaires," and Petrie has done the same for English readers in his "Egyptian Tales," first and second series.

Papyrus. It was the *cyperus papyrus*, a plant not now found in Egypt, from which the papyrus for writing on was made. It grew in marshy places, and the cultivation of it seems to have been a government monopoly. That there were other varieties of this useful plant seems evident from the references to it in the classic authors. Strabo calls the first kind the *hieratic byblus*, to distinguish it from the common sort. Pliny says it was cultivated chiefly in the Sebennytic Nome. According to him, the triangular stalk of the plant was 15 ft. high, and it was crowned "as with a thyrsus." Every part of the plant was used. The root, which was large and thick, provided fuel and material for making certain utensils, and out of the stem were made small boats. Sails, mats, rope, bedding, and clothes were all made of it, besides the famous writing material. Herodotus tells us that the young shoots were gathered, "topped," and cooked for food, being considered a delicacy. The papyrus now growing in Sicily is said to be identical with the Egyptian papyrus.

The papyrus upon which the scribes wrote their books was prepared by removing the outer rind and then slicing the stem into very thin layers. Several widths of this were laid side by side, other layers put on across these with a thin solution of some unknown adhesive substance between, then the whole was pressed and dried. The result, when a good plant of papyrus had been used, was a very fair surface for writing upon. The specimens that have come down to us vary in colour from a rather dark brown to a dark cream colour, and are of different textures. (*See* PAPYRI.)

A conventionalized form of the plant was frequently used for decorative purposes, and figures largely on tomb and temple walls. It was also a symbol of **Lower Egypt.**

Paraschistes. The man who, with an "Ethiopian stone," made the slit in the side of the deceased in order to withdraw the intestines before embalming the body.

Pasebkhanu I. A king of the XXIst Dynasty, brother of Men-kheper-Rā, high priest of Amen, and son of Painezem I. He was king of Tanis while Shashanq sat on the throne at Bubastis. He is chiefly known from the wall which he built round Tanis (*q.v.*), the bricks of which are stamped with his cartouche.

Pasht. *See* PAKHT.

Pens. *See* REED.

Pentaur. A scribe who has become celebrated as the writer of the great epic poem of Egypt. But he was probably not the author, as was for long supposed, but only the transcriber of the papyrus copy. (*See* POEM OF PENTAUR.)

Pepi, *Meri-Rā*. Third king of Dynasty VIth, cir.

3467 B.C. From the immense number of inscriptions, graffiti, and monuments bearing his name, we gather that Pepi must have been a vigorous monarch. From the inscription of Unàs (*q.v.*), which is the earliest historical document of any length, we learn that in this reign the Egyptians began to make expeditions for conquest and travel. Pepi's pyramid, Men-nefer, is at Sakkâra.

Persea tree. This tree, called in Egyptian Àst, was either the *balanites Aegyptiaca* (Raffenan-Delile) the Arab *lebakh* or the *mimusops Schimeperi* (Schweinfurth). It was one of the principal sacred trees of ancient

Egypt. It frequently occurs in scenes in which the god Thoth, or the goddess Safekh, is seen inscribing the

Persea Tree.

name of some king, who stands near, on its leaves, thus securing to him everlasting life.

Persian Dynasty. Cambyses at the battle of Pelusium defeated Psammetichus III. and took possession of Egypt. He is said to have caused the destruction of many of the wonderful monuments of Egypt, and made himself particularly odious to the Egyptians by killing their new Apis bull. But another account shows that he restored the temple of Neith at Saïs and performed the rites as other Egyptian kings. He was succeeded by Darius Hystaspes, who tried to improve the condition of the people and country. He established a coinage, completed the Red Sea to Mediterranean canal, and improved the system of taxation. Towards the end of his reign Egypt again made itself independent, but was again subdued by Xerxes I. His successor, Artaxerxes I., had great trouble there, but finally conquered the Egyptians and their Greek mercenaries. He was followed by Xerxes II. and Darius II., under which latter king the Egyptians threw off the Persian yoke in 400 B.C.; but it was but for a short time. In 340, Nectanebo, the last native Egyptian ruler, fled before the army of Artaxerxes III., and under Arses and Darius III., Egypt remained in Persian hands until the coming of Alexander the Great.

Phakussa. The Greek name for *Pekes*, capital of the twentieth nome of Lower Egypt, the modern Saft el Henneh. Chief deity, Sopt. This nome is probably the site of the Goshen of Scripture.

Pharaoh ⌑, *Per aā,* lit. "the great house." The title by which all the monarchs of Egypt were designated, and not as some think the name of the king. (*See* Hastings, Dic. of Bible and **S.B.A. Proc.** vol. xxiii. pt. 2.)

Pharaoh Necho. *See* NEKAU.

Phœnix. *See* BENNU.

Physicians. According to Herodotus there were specialists among the Egyptian doctors—"some for diseases of the eyes, others for the head, or the teeth, or the stomach, or for internal diseases." But in early times it is probable that there were the two classes of doctors, those who had been through what training it was possible to give in the priestly schools, and those who simply pretended to cure by the use of amulets and magical formulae. The medical papyri (*q.v.*) are about equally composed of practical remedies and magic. The best instructed physicians knew little of anatomy, religious scruples preventing dissection. Thoth was the god who presided over this branch of science. He was called the first physician and the

first surgeon. Bone-setting seemed, however, to have
been under the protection of Sekhet, fractures being
cured by intercession with her.

The royal physicians enjoyed considerable distinction. A certain king Sahurā presented his chief
physician with a costly " false door " for his tomb, the
making of which he personally superintended.

Piānkhi. The Ethiopian king who lived at Napata
during the eighth century B.C., and conquered Egypt.
The celebrated "Stela of Piānkhi," a granite block
covered with an inscription telling of his victories in
Egypt, was set up at Gebel Barkel in Nubia. His
queen Ameniritis is well known from her beautiful
alabaster statue now in the Cairo Museum.

Picture frame. Until the present time there has
been but one specimen only found, and that was discovered by Petrie when excavating in the cemetery of
Hawara in 1889. It is made of painted wood and
contains a portrait; the corners are joined with
mortises and tenons. There is a slit running down
both the top sides, evidently for the purpose of allow-
ing a sliding cover to pass; and as a sheet of clear glass
has been discovered among the ruins of Tanis, it is not
impossible that the picture may have been covered
with that material. This unique specimen is now in
the British Museum.

Pig. This animal figures but rarely on the
monuments, and was probably not used for food.
Herodotus speaks of seeing a herd of pigs "treading
in the seed." (*See* AGRICULTURE.) From the "Book of
the Dead " (*q.v.*) we learn that Set, the enemy of Osiris,
once took the form of a pig.

Pigments. As far back as the Vth Dynasty seven
colours were in use; yellow, red, blue, brown, black,
white and green; and in the XVIIIth Dynasty, three

yellows, three browns, two blues, two reds, and two greens; making about fourteen or sixteen different tints. The composition of the chief colours was as follows: White—sulphate of lime, or gypsum; Yellow —ochre, or sulphate of arsenic, our modern orpiment; Red—ochre, or cinnabar; Dark Red—oxide of iron with a small admixture of sand; Blue—pulverized lapis lazuli, or a cheaper kind from glass coloured by silicate of copper and powdered; Pink—sulphate of lime coloured by some organic substance, probably madder; Black—from calcined animal bones.

The colours were so well prepared, that to this day much of the work of Egyptian artists retains almost all its original brilliancy. The pigments were mixed as required with water and a little gum tragacanth. Varnish was not used until about the time of the XIXth Dynasty. It was probably made from the gum of some kind of acacia. This method, however, was found to be unsuitable, as it both cracked and darkened the paintings, and so was discontinued about the close of the same Dynasty. (*See* COBALT.)

Pithom of Exodus i. 11., the *Pa Tum* of ancient Egypt. Ruins of this town have been identified in excavations at the modern Tel el Maskhutah, by Edouard Naville. The name has been found on a statue and on the great tablet of Ptolemy Philadelphus discovered at this spot. The name is also written *Ha Tum*, or *Ha-neter Tum*, and was known through the lists of nomes to be the capital of the eighth nome of Lower Egypt. It is situated about ten miles west of the southern end of Lake Timsah.

In all probability Pithom was built by Ramses II., no monuments more ancient than those which bear his mark having been unearthed. There is no royal stamp on the bricks. Remains of the XXIInd Dynasty—Shashanq I. and Osorkon II.—have been found. Nectanebo I. also built at Pithom. In the time of Ptolemy Philadelphus it was the starting-point of commercial expeditions to the Red Sea. Various

papyri associate Pithom with a region called *Thuku*,
or *Thuket;* ⟨hieroglyphs⟩ ; ⟨hieroglyphs⟩ ; (Pap. Anastasi vi. 4,
line 13) which has been identified with the Hebrew
Succoth (Exodus xiii. 20.) Succoth was the district
in which the Israelites encamped, and in which the
town Pithom was built.

Under the Greek Dynasty, Pithom became
Heroöpolis, a name abridged into Ero by the Romans.

The portions of the walls and chambers that have
been excavated are of a very substantial character, indicating a good epoch. Such is the construction of these
chambers, that M. Naville says: "I believe them to have
been built for no other purpose than that of storehouses,
or granaries, into which the Pharaohs gathered the pro-
visions necessary for armies about to cross the desert,
or even for caravans and travellers which were on the
road to Syria. It is also very likely that the Ptolemies
used them as warehouses in the trade with Africa,
which took place through the Heroöpolitan Gulf."
("The Store-City of Pithom," by Edouard Naville.)

See statue of Ankh-renp-nefer in British Museum
Southern Egyptian Gallery, No. 1007.

Planets. *See* ASTRONOMY.

Poem of Pentaur. The name which was given by
E. de Rougé to the great epic of Egypt. He studied
it from the papyrus copy which was made by a scribe
called Pentaur and hence he concluded that this was
the name of the author. The "poem" is found on the
walls of the temples at Karnak, Abydos, Abu Simbel,
and Luxor. It was first discovered among the Sallier
Papyri (No. 3) of the British Museum. Its subject is
the campaign of Ramses II. against the Kheta
(Hittites?). The style is most graphic, as if the story
were told by an eye-witness. The most dramatic part
describes the hero Ramses left almost alone among
the enemy, whose serried ranks of chariots, each con-

taining three men, seem completely to enclose him.
Then Ramses calls upon his father Amen, " What are
these Asiatics to thy heart? Amen will humiliate
those who know not the god. Have I not consecrated
innumerable offerings unto thee? . . . My many
soldiers have forsaken me. . . . But I find that
Amen is more to me than a million soldiers, than a
hundred thousand charioteers." Amen hears the cry,
and tells his son that he is with him and will help him.
The enemy retreat in terror, recognizing the invincible
hand of a god against them. Then the coward army
returns to the king, he reproaches them, and describes
his gallant action and how his favourite horses, "Victory
in Thebes " and " Nuret Satisfied," only were left to
him. (For translation, see " Records of the Past," first
series, vol. ii.) (*See* POETRY.)

Poetry. In the sense of rhyming lines Egyptian
literature has no poetry. But a distinct rhythm is
found in some of the hymns and eulogies, and much
poetic feeling. Their similes show imagination and
observation of nature, and they were not above the
use of alliteration. The love-sick maiden says, " What
is sweet to the mouth is to me as the gall of birds;
thy breath alone can comfort my heart." One love
song has every verse commencing with the name of a
flower. The great Egyptian epic is the so-called poem
of Pentaur (*q.v.*). It has in part " a form with which
we are familiar in Hebrew poetry, the so-called parallel-
ism of the phrases; two short sentences following
each other, and corresponding in arrangement, and
also as a rule in purport." Many poems were written
to be accompanied by the harp, as we so frequently
see in the tombs. It is from tomb walls also that we
have those little lyrics or ballads which are of the
people. We give one example :—

" Your shepherd is in the water with the fish,
   He talks with the sheath fish, he salutes the pike
  From the west ! your shepherd is a shepherd from the west."

Portraits. The introduction of painted portraits into Egypt dates from about 130 A.D., and succeeded to the moulded and stucco cartonnages with which the heads and busts of the mummies were at that period covered. The portraits come from the cemetery of Hawara in the Fayûm, which was excavated by Mr. Petrie in 1889, and show a strong Greek influence. This is to be accounted for by the fact that there was at this period a large Greek colony in the Fayûm. The portraits are executed in colours, which have been ground to a very fine powder, and were then rubbed up with heated wax. This was applied with the brush to a panel of cedar or fine wood, varying in thickness from $\frac{1}{16}$ to $\frac{1}{4}$ inch, and about 9 by 17 inches in size. The portrait was laid over the face of the mummy, and kept in place by the bandages. From the conventional style of these portraits it is thought that they were executed after death, and finished from memory. There are good specimens of these Graeco-Egyptian pictures in the National Gallery and the British Museum.

Praefects. For the best list of Praefects of Egypt see Professor Milne's "Egypt under Roman Rule."

Pre-historic. A term applied by some Egyptologists to all objects which they believe to be anterior to the 1st Dynasty. The reasons for considering them to be of this remote period are hardly sufficiently cogent at present to permit of this definition being accepted in all cases. It must be remembered that the dynastic Egyptians were not aboriginal, and that traces of what were in all probability the native races survived until long after the commencement of the Pharaonic period. It is therefore more than probable that many of the so-called pre-historic objects belong not to the ante-Pharaonic, but to the aboriginal inhabitants of the country.

Priests. The Egyptian priesthood seems to have

been a very large and elastic order.   Kings and governors, queens and princesses, all held priestly offices,
and below those of high rank there were numberless
grades of officials in connection with the various
temples and services of the different gods.   The ritual
and services of the temples were elaborate, and there
were perpetually recurring festivals which entailed a
great amount of labour.   From the earliest times we
find that the priesthood was of importance, but the
power of the priestly faction gradually increased during
the Middle Empire, and under the New Empire it
forms one of the most important elements of the kingdom.   There were many priestesses, whose chief
function seems to have been to sing and recite.
Among priestly titles the following are the best known :
—The *Sam* priest was the chief priest at Memphis.
The *Hersheshta* was the diviner.   The *Kher-ḥeb* was
a master of ceremonies.   The *Setem*, the "prophet,"
the "purifier," and the "divine father," all ranked
above the ordinary priest.

Prisse Papyrus. *See* PTAH-ḤETEP ; PRECEPTS OF.

Psammetichus I. *Uaḥ-àb-Rā*.   The founder of the

XXVIth Dynasty at Saïs, B.C. 666-612.   He married
Shep-en-àpt, the daughter and heiress of the Ethiopian king Piānkhi and his queen Àmeniritis, and
brought Patoris to her husband as a wedding gift.
Psammetichus made a successful military expedition
into Nubia ; but his reign is chiefly remarkable for
the revival of art, which flourished under his fostering
care.   Saïte art shows a strong Hellenic influence,
though the ideas are the same as those which prevailed under the ancient Empire.   This king employed
Greek mercenaries in his army, and permitted Greeks
to establish themselves in the Delta.

Psammetichus III., *Ānkh-ka-en-Rā*, XXVIth Dynasty,

B.C. 525. Son of Åāḥmes II., who gallantly resisted
the invasion of his country by Cambyses. After a
stern resistance, first at Pelusium, and then at Memphis, he was taken prisoner, and put to death within
six months of his accession.

Psychostasia. It was an accepted belief from the
very earliest ages that every one must be brought into
the Hall of Double Truth, and there be judged by
Osiris for their course of conduct during life.

The soul, after first making the negative confession
before the Forty-Two Assessors of the Dead, is conducted into the presence of Osiris. The heart or
conscience, in the form of a small vase, is placed in the
scale opposite to the feather of Truth ; upon the beam
of the balance sits the little cynocephalus (*q.v.*), the
attendant of Thoth. Ånpu is usually standing close by
to examine or test the indicator. Above is seen the soul
of the deceased resting upon the top of a pylon (?).
Near at hand stands Shai, or Destiny, and behind him
Meskhent and Renenet, the two goddesses who presided over the birth and education of children. Beyond is Thoth, " the scribe of the gods," reed-pen and
palette in hand, ready to inscribe the result of the
weighing of the heart. Behind him is a hideous composite animal, Āmām, with the body of a lioness, the
head and forequarters of a crocodile, and the hind-
quarters of a hippopotamus ; she is called the " Devourer of the Wicked." The soul is then taken by
the hand by Horus, and conducted to Osiris, who is
seated on a throne beneath a canopy ; before him are
the " four children of Horus," standing upon an opening lotus flower ; and behind him are Isis and Nephthys.
Judgment is then pronounced, and the deceased is
either permitted to join the cycle of the gods in the

Fields of Peace, or else is seized upon and consumed by the "Devourer of the Wicked." There are a great many representations of the judgment scene extant, all of them varying slightly in detail. The papyrus of Ani in the British Museum is one of the finest in Europe, and there is a splendid bas-relief of it upon the walls of the temple of Dêr el Medineh at Thebes.

Ptah. In Memphis Ptah was considered the oldest of the gods. He is called, "Father of the mighty fathers, father of the beginnings, he who created the sun egg and the moon egg," "the creator of his own image." With Sekhet and Im-ḥetep he formed the triad worshipped at Memphis, where a splendid temple was built to him. He is represented with a mummied body, a close-fitting cap, no head-dress, and with a curious unexplained tassel hanging out of the back of his neck. In his hands he holds a sceptre, which terminates in the signs for power, life, and stability. His name signifies "architect, framer, constructor." One legend associates him with Khnemu in the work of creation under the commands of Thoth. He is said to have established everlasting justice upon earth. The Greeks compared him to Hephaistos, the Latin Vulcan. Ptah is found in conjunction with other gods, the most important fusion being with Seker Osiris.

Ptah.

Ptah-ḥetep, Precepts of. This work is contained in the famous "Prisse Papyrus," which has been called "The oldest book in the world." (*See* PAPYRI.) It dates back to the Vth Dynasty, and yet "appeals to the authority of the ancients." Parts of it are extremely difficult to translate, although the general purport of the text can be gathered. But other parts are more easily understood. The moral teaching is of the same kind as that found in the Book of Proverbs. The pious son is extolled, and duty to parents and superiors inculcated. The path of the virtuous is shown to be advantageous, and by contrast the evil of disobedience, pride, laziness, intemperance, and other vices is pointed out. For translation, see "Records of the Past."

Ptah-Seker-Osiris. A form of the god Ptah under which he symbolized the inert form of Osiris, the mummy with its possibilities and certainty of resurrection. Large numbers of Ptah-Seker-Osiris figures have been found. They are made of wood, and mounted on a little pedestal, which projects some distance in front. This pedestal and the statuette itself are frequently hollow, and contain papyri inscribed with certain chapters from the "Book of the Dead." The figures and pedestals are gaily painted, and are usually inscribed with the ordinary prayer formula for sepulchral meals.

Ptolemies. At the death of Alexander the Great in 323 B.C. his empire was divided among his generals, Egypt falling to the lot of his favourite and familiar companion, Ptolemy, a man who had risen from an obscure position in the army. He founded a dynasty which lasted nearly three hundred years, ending with the death of Cleopatra in 30 B.C. The history of the fourteen Ptolemies and the seven Cleopatras is a record of small campaigns, murders, and immorality. At the same time there was great literary and scientific activity during the early part of the period. Many temples were built, the well-preserved remains of which form some of the finest examples of architecture extant ; the style of art had, however, altered considerably from that of Pharaonic times. At Philae, Kom Ombo, Edfu, and Dendera there are Ptolemaic temples. (*See* CLEOPATRA.)

Punt, called also **Ta-neter**, the "land of God."
This region is identified by Maspero, Mariette, and
Brugsch, as that part of the African coast which ex-
tends from the Straits of Bab-el-Mandeb to Cape
Gardafui. It was a country rich in balsam and in-
cense-bearing trees, in precious woods, lapis lazuli,
ivory and amber. To this "blessed land" Queen
Hatshepsut sent an expedition, building and equipping
a fleet of five large vessels for the purpose. On their
arrival they were received in the most friendly way by
Parihu, Prince of Punt, his wife Ati, and their daughter
and two sons. After an interchange of gifts, the fleet
returned to Egypt, laden with odoriferous sycomore
trees—identified by Mariette with the "myrrh tree"
of Pliny—ivory, skins, logs of ebony, apes, gold dust,
gold and metal rings, and heaps of the precious gum.
The whole story of this expedition is vividly depicted
upon the walls of the great temple of Dêr el Bahri.

Pylon. The colossal gateway forming the façade of a
temple. It consisted of a large, ordinary entrance,
with enormous masses of masonry on either side,
having sloping faces and an overhanging cornice.
Sometimes these two massive towers contained small
chambers, sometimes only a staircase. On the face
of each were four vertical grooves, in which were held
great wooden masts, bearing floating streamers of
different colours. Inscriptions and sculptured pictures
covered the sloping fronts (*see* PENTAUR), and
statues or obelisks were placed before them. The
statues, of which there were four or six, were sometimes of enormous dimensions. They represented the
royal founder of the temple.

Pyramids. There are remains of at least seventy
more or less ruined pyramids on the long plateau,
extending from Abu Roash in the north to Medûm in
the south. These divide themselves into groups, viz.,
Abu Roash, Gîzeh, Abusîr, Sakkâra, Dahshur, Lisht,
and the Fayûm group, that of Medûm standing alone.

But of all these less than twenty have been identified as tombs of different kings. Many theories have been advanced as to their age, purpose, method of construction, etc., and much excavation and measuring have proved that they were built between the period of the Ist and XIIth Dynasties, solely as tombs for the preservation of royal mummies. The method of construction has been a puzzle to the engineering mind since classic times. Herodotus and Diodorus both record what had been told to them on the point, but neither theory is conclusive. It has been recently proved that it would be quite possible with the unlimited manual labour at the command of the Pharaohs to construct a pyramid without any complex or elaborate machinery.* The finer examples are built of nummulitic limestone from the quarries of Turah and Masarah on the other side of the river. Others, as some at Dahshur, were built of mud brick, only the passages and chambers inside being of limestone. In some cases only the accidental discovery of such chambers has led to the knowledge that the mound of detritus above was once a pyramid. The great pyramid at Gîzeh in its original state presented four smooth surfaces to the beholder, as it was entirely faced with granite and limestone blocks most beautifully joined. But the whole of this outer casing has disappeared, the place having for centuries served as a quarry. The passages inside were arranged with an intricacy designed to foil the efforts of plunderers. In spite of the great care thus taken to conceal the mummy, the pyramid was opened many times, by Persians, Romans, and Arabs, and when investigated in more modern times nothing remained in the chambers but a lidless sarcophagus without inscription. In some of the chambers above the name of Khufu was discovered, conclusively proving that this was the tomb of the second king of the IVth Dynasty. Of the two other pyramids that

* See "Mechanical Triumphs of the Ancient Egyptians." Commander Barber, U.S.N.

form the Gîzeh groups, the larger is that of Khafra or
Khephren, the other, that of Men-kau-Râ or Mycerinus.
The pyramids at Abusîr are the tombs of Sahu-Râ,
Râ-en-user and other Vth Dynasty kings. At Sakkâra
are the tombs of Unás, Tetá, Pepi I., Mer-en-Râ,
Pepi II.; at Lisht, that of Usertsen I.; at Medûm that
of Sneferu; in the Fayûm, those of Usertsen II. and
Amen-em-hât III. of the XIIth Dynasty. There are
also pyramids at Thebes, el Qullah, near Napata in
Ethiopia, and at Meroë

Pyramid Texts. This phrase refers to the inscriptions in the pyramid tombs of Unás, Tetá, Pepi I.,
Pepi II., and Seker-em-sa-f. These long, exquisitely
carved inscriptions contain various chapters from the
" Book of the Dead." They have been published by
Maspero in the *Recueil de Travaux*, with a French translation. The form of the language differs greatly from
that found in later times, and is more difficult to
translate.

Q

Qebhsennuf or **Kebhsenuf.** *See* CANOPIC JARS

Quarries. The chief quarries for limestone are at
Tûrah, and Masârah, nearly opposite to the site of
Memphis. Sandstone was chiefly quarried at Silsilis
and Gebel Abû Fedeh; granite at Hammamât and
Aswân; porphyry at Hammamât, and alabaster at
Hat Nûb.

R

Rā. The creator of gods, men, and the world. According to some inscriptions he was more ancient even than the firmament. The sun, emblem of life, light, and fertility, is his symbol. The chief seat of the worship of Rā was Ånnu, the Hebrew On or Beth-shemesh, the Greek Heliopolis. He is usually depicted as a hawk-headed human being crowned with the sun's disk and uraeus, and grasping the *user* sceptre in his hand.

Rā.

Ramessēum. The name given to the great temple of Ramses II., built on the plain of Thebes, on the western bank of the Nile. It served as a mortuary chapel to his tomb in the valley behind (*see* Tomb). The Greeks called it the Memnonium, by a corruption of the Egytian word *mennu*, which word they observed frequently in the inscriptions, turning the simple word meaning "monument" or "memorial" into a proper name. They also called it the tomb of Osymandias, who, according to Diodorus, was User-maāt-Rā, that is Ramses II. The walls are covered with inscriptions and illustrations, many of which relate the story of the king's wars against the Kheta.

Ramses I., *Men-peḥtet Rā*, Dynasty XIX., cir.

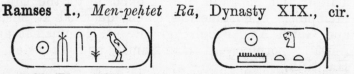

B.C. 1400 (B). With the incoming of this new dynasty came also the revival of the ancient worship of Ámen, and Thebes became once more the seat of government. The rise of the powerful Kheta people became a source of danger to the Egyptian kingdom. The fame of Ramses I. rests in the fact that his son, Seti I., and his grandson, Ramses II., were two of the most celebrated of the long line of Pharaohs.

Ramses II., *User-maāt-Rā, Setep-en-Rā,* Dynasty

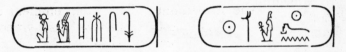

XIX., cir. B.C. 1333 (P.). The Sesothis of Manetho and Sesostris of the Greeks, and one of the most celebrated of all the Egyptian kings. The first care of this monarch on ascending the throne was to finish the beautiful temple of Abydos begun by his father, Seti I. He added also to the temples of Karnak and Luxor, restored that of Ptah at Memphis, and built as a lasting memorial of his fame the rock-cut temple of Abû Simbel, and the Ramessēum, before which he placed the largest colossal statues that are known. In Nubia are also many of his buildings. This king did not hesitate to appropriate the work of his predecessors to himself, and both on temples and statues their names may be seen chiselled out, and his own cut over them.

During the reign of Ramses II., the powerful Kheta, under their king, Kheta-sar, waged war against Egypt, Kadesh being the rallying-point; and, although in the Poem of Pentaur (*q.v.*) the king's courage and prowess are loudly sung, he comes out of the war but a very doubtful conqueror. Peace was ratified by the marriage of the Kheta king's daughter with the Pharaoh. In Syria, however, the Egyptian army was more successful, and there are long lists of the conquered peoples to be seen upon Ramses II.'s monuments at Thebes. From an inscription at Kûban it is clear that the working of the Nubian gold mines, which was begun during the reign of Seti I., was continued under his successor.

The "treasure cities" of Pithom and Ramses, built by the forced labour of the Israelites, date from this reign; and Zaān or Pa-Ramessu, became one of the capitals of the kingdom.

Ramses II. is by most Egyptologists considered to be the Pharaoh of the oppression; he reigned sixty-seven years, and was succeeded by his fourteenth son, Mer-en-Ptah. The mummy of this Pharaoh is in the Cairo Museum.

Ramses III., *User-maāt-Rā*, the Rhampsinitus of

the Greeks, Dynasty XX., cir. B.C. 1200. The reign of this king marks an era of great commercial prosperity for Egypt; he is more celebrated for his buildings and his rich gifts to the already existing temples of Abydos, Heliopolis (On), and Thebes, than for any great military victories. The peace of his reign was disturbed by the famous Harem conspiracy described in the Turin, the Lee, Rollin, and Amherst papyri.

Ramessides, the. The name usually given to the numerous kings of that name—from Ramses III. to XIII.—who occupied the throne of Egypt during the XXth Dynasty, cir. B.C. 1200—1100. Of them there is little to say but that in their hands the greatness of the country steadily declined, and the power of the high priests of Amen at Thebes steadily rose.

Rā-t. A goddess not frequently met with. She represents the feminine principle of Rā, and was rather an abstract idea of the priests than a distinct deity. She is represented as a woman with the sun's disk and cow-horns on her head, and also as a uraeus with the same head-dress.

Razors. Bronze razors, somewhat resembling

English ones, have been found, and specimens may be seen in museums.

Reed. The Egyptians used reeds for writing. The ends were not cut, but bruised to a brush-like point, in early times. Later they were cut to a pen-shape like the reed-pens now used for writing Arabic. They were about ten inches long.

Rekh-ma-rā. The name of a Governor of Thebes under Amen-ḥetep II. of the XVIIIth Dynasty. His tomb at Shêkh abd el Qurna at Thebes is exceedingly fine and interesting, as showing tributaries bringing offerings.

Religion. No one name can be given to the systems of religious thought that obtained in Egypt during the four thousand years of its history as a people. It is probable that there occurred phases of monotheism, henotheism, pantheism, and in the latest, corrupt time, even polytheism.

That the ancient Egyptians had a clear and precise conception of one supreme Being is a fact agreed to by all serious Egyptologists. This Being is called the Neter (hieroglyphic ⌐), a word signifying power and corresponding to the Hebrew El. References to the Neter are constant in Egyptian literature, where he is spoken of in terms which indicate unmistakably the monotheistic attitude of the writer. " Give thyself to God, keep thyself continually for God," the young man was told. " Bring up thy son in the love of God " is one of the maxims of Ptah-ḥetep (*q.v.*)

But beside the doctrine of the one God, the priests also taught the people of many gods or powers. These gods, says Renouf, " represent the real or imaginary powers of the universe." They were simply mythical personages to begin with, around whom in time clustered many mythological legends. The phenomena personified were chiefly those of regular and perpetual

recurrence—the sunrise and sunset, the return of day
and night, the battle between light and darkness.

Ren, *lit.* Name. The Egyptians considered the name
to be a most important part of a human being—in fact
they practically looked upon it as a separate entity.
A man's name was thought to exist after him, and to
be known in heaven.

Renenet.

Renenet or **Ranen**. The goddess of
good fortune, the harvest goddess. In
the "Book of the Dead" she is usually
connected with Shái and Meskhent. She
is represented with a human body with
the uraeus for head, and sometimes with
a head-dress of two plumes and other
divine insignia.

Renpit or **Repit**. A goddess representing the personified year, *renpit* being
the Egyptian word for year. She belonged to the Memphite cycle of gods.
Sometimes *Ta-urt* and *Hathor* are identified with her. She is pictured in human
form, the symbol on her head being a
notched palm branch. Frequently she
carries a long notched branch in her
hand.

Rert. A late form of the goddess
Ta-urt (*q.v.*). The word *rert* is merely
the Egyptian for hippopotamus. She
is spoken of as dwelling in "the
House of Suckling."

Reshpu. A god imported from Asia
in later times, probably the same as
the Phoenician war god, Resef. He
is called "great god, lord of heaven,
ruler of eternity, lord of might in the

Renpit.

midst of the divine circle." He is represented with
a Semitic face and natural beard, and instead of the

Rert.   Reshpu.

uraeus wears the miniature head of a gazelle on his
forehead.

Rhampsinitus. The Greek name for Ramses III.
Herodotus, however, in one of his numerous mistakes,
places him before Khufu (Cheops).

Rings. Many have been found in gold, silver,
bronze, iron, enamel, or frit and stone. Some of the
designs are very charming. Some consist of a single
wire with a scarab set so that it can turn round.

Rohes. A form of Sebek worshipped in the Fayûm.

Roman Emperors. Between the years B.C. 30 and
A.D. 640 Egypt formed part of the Roman Empire.
The emperors governed the country through a praefect.
It was an uneventful period on the whole. The emperors had their names translated into Egyptian, and
many of their cartouches may be seen on the walls which
they built or restored, those most frequently occurring
being Tiberius and Claudius. (*See* PRAEFECTS.)

Rosetta Stone. A slab of black basalt, bearing a trilingual inscription, which has proved the key to the decipherment of the hieroglyphs; for it is inscribed with a decree written first in hieroglyphs, then in demotic, and thirdly in Greek. It was found near the Rosetta mouth of the Nile by a French artillery officer named Boussard, in 1798, and at the capitulation of Alexandria came into the possession of the British Government, who in 1802 placed it in the British Museum (Southern Egyptian Gallery). Part of the top has been broken off, also a portion of the right-hand lower corner, so that it now measures 3 ft. 9 ins. by 2 ft. 4½ ins. by 11 ins. There are 14 lines of hieroglyphs, 32 lines of demotic, and 54 lines of Greek. The subject is a decree of the priests of Memphis conferring divine honours on Ptolemy V., Epiphanes (B.C. 195). For translations see "Inscriptio Rosettana," by Brugsch, Berlin, 1851; "L'Inscription hiéroglyphique de Rosette," by Chabas, Paris, 1867. For reproduction, see Lepsius, Auswahl, Bl. 18.

Rouge. Rouge was in use among the Egyptians as an article for the toilettes of ladies of fashion, for the dead, and for the statues of the gods. A papyrus in the Turin Museum contains an amusing caricature of a lady, mirror in hand, rougeing her lips. So long ago as the Old Empire two sorts of rouge are mentioned in the lists of offerings for the dead; and according to an Abydos ritual the priest of the day on first entering the temple was to incense the statue of the god and then proceed to commence its toilette by removing the old rouge from the face.

Rutennu of the East, was the old Egyptian name for Syria. An Upper Ruten or Rutennu is spoken of in distinction from the Lower Rutennu. The country and people figure largely in inscriptions of the XVIIIth Dynasty, Thothmes III. having warred against them.

S

Safekh. The goddess of learning, or perhaps more properly of writing. She is usually represented standing by the sacred tree of Heliopolis, on the leaves of which she is writing the name of the king, thus endowing him with eternal life. In such a scene Thoth usually stands behind her. She was venerated at Memphis from the earliest times. The symbol of the palm-leaf circled by the inverted horns is peculiar to her. She carries either a notched palm branch or a reed and palette. (*See* SESHTA.)

Safekh.

Sāhu. The spiritual body, which "shall not see corruption." In a vignette in the "Book of the Dead" it is figured as a beautiful lily springing up from the *khat* or corruptible body. (*See* KHAT.)

Sahu-Rā.  The second king of Dynasty V., cir. 3693 B.C., reigned thirteen years.

Saïs. Greek name for *Sait*, capital of the fifth nome of Lower Egypt, the modern Sa el Hagar. Chief deity Nit.

Saïtes. The fifth nome of Lower Egypt. The local deity was Nit.

Sakkâra. A modern Arab village standing on the site of the ancient necropolis of Memphis. The principal

monuments at Sakkâra are the "Pyramid of Degrees"
or "Stepped Pyramid," the "Mastabat-el-Farûn," the
Serapēum, and the tombs of Thi and Ptah-ḥetep.

Sakkâra, the Tablet of. A stela of great historic
interest discovered by M. Mariette during the excavations at Sakkâra, and now in the Cairo Museum. It was
found in the tomb of a priest named Tunari, and represents him paying homage in the name of Ramses
II. to a series of forty-seven kings, many of whom
belong to the first six dynasties. It agrees closely
with the list of kings given on the Tablet of Abydos.
Mer-ba-pen, the sixth king of Dynasty I., is the first
mentioned on the Tablet of Sakkâra.

Sam-ta, or **Sam-taui.** "Uniter of the two worlds,"
a name given to Thothmes III. after his accession.

Sandals. Formed generally of papyrus, palm bast,
or leather. They were fastened on with two straps,
one passing over the instep and the other between the
toes. It was not etiquette to wear them in the
presence of a superior. The use of sandals was almost
entirely confined to men.

Sarcophagi. The sarcophagus was the outer stone
casing in which the mummy, with its one, two, three,
or more wooden coffins, was placed. Several may still
be seen *in situ* in the tombs, and many have been
brought to museums. The workmanship displayed in
the fashioning of them is unsurpassable even in these
days. They were usually made of the finest and
hardest kind of stone procurable. Various kinds of
granite, basalt, and breccia were used, also limestone,
and in the case of Seti I., a beautiful semi-transparent
alabaster. The design varied with the dynasties. At
first it was rectangular, with a flat or vaulted lid.
From the VIIth to XVIIth Dynasty time the custom
of using sarcophagi seems to have been in abeyance.

In the XVIIIth Dynasty we find them made in the form of a mummy. Some in succeeding dynasties were shaped like a cartouche; then in the XXVIth rectangular shape again comes into favour. From this period up to Ptolemaic times the numerous examples were massive, finely worked and decorated. The inscriptions on early ones were short, recording the names and titles of deceased and the *Seten-ḥetep tā* formula (*q.v.*). Occasionally, however, the sides were sculptured to represent a building with doors and various openings. Later the decorations became more and more elaborate, usually incised or in relief *en creux*, but sometimes entirely in relief. Scenes and long extracts from the "Book of the Dead" form the main subject of the decorations.

Sati. One of the Elephantiné triad of gods. She was wife of Khnemu, who with his other wife Anūkit formed the triad. She is picturesquely spoken of as the archeress who shoots forth the current (i.e. the cataract) straight and swift as an arrow. Little is known about her, but on the island of Sehêl there have been found the remains of a temple to the two goddesses. She is mentioned in some texts as the daughter of Rā, and also as a form of Isis, and is represented wearing the vulture head-dress, and the crown of Upper Egypt with the cow's horns.

Sati.

Scarab. This is an amulet made in the form of the beetle known as Scarabeus sacer. It is the symbol of the god Kheperä, i.e. "he who turns" or "rolls," for the conception was that Khepera caused the sun to move across the sky as the beetle causes its ball to roll. A scarab inscribed with the 30th (B) chapter of the "Book of the Dead" took the place of the heart

in the body of the deceased. The prescribed form for
such heart-scarabs was gold plated, with a silver ring
for attachment. Scarabs have been found in great
number and variety. They were made in amethyst,
crystal, lapis lazuli, carnelian, granite, and many
other stones. The majority were composed of
faïence.

Scarabeus Sacer. A large beetle of black metallic
colour common in Egypt. It is remarkable for the
peculiar position and shape of the hind legs, which are
placed very far apart and at the extreme end of the
body. This is to enable the insect to roll the ball of
refuse containing its eggs into some place of safety.
At first these balls are soft and shapeless, but as
they are pushed along by the scarab's hindlegs they
become firm and round, and increase in size until
they are sometimes an inch and a half in diameter.
This insect is looked upon by the Arabs as an emblem
of fertility.

Sceptre. There was no one sceptre proper to
royalty. Kings and gods are alike represented holding
the *user* sceptre with the greyhound (?) head, and though
goddesses are more frequently shown holding one
with a lotus flower at the top, they also often carry
the other.

Scorpion. This insect must have been fairly
common in ancient times, for numbers of magical
formulae have been found for protection from its sting.
It was the emblem of the goddess Selk, who is
represented with the scorpion on her head.

Scribes. To be a scribe was the great desire of the
ambitious Egyptian youth, almost any rank could be
attained by a clever member of the profession. The
most frequently-recurring phrase in the scholars'
exercises of the New Empire was, "One has only to

be a scribe, for the scribe takes the lead of all," and
to a certain extent such an one was more his own
master than the ordinary man, for he was exempt
from military service and forced labour. There were
numberless grades in the profession, from the mere
registrar of his employer's cattle to the literary man
like Pentaur (*q.v.*). The education of a scribe was
not obtained at any public institution. After having
learnt the rudiments of reading and writing, probably
in a little school like the modern Arab " Kuttab," he
was taken into his father's office or apprenticed to
some other scribe. Then if he improved, if his hand-
writing became fine and neat, if he made himself in-
dispensable to his master, he might become rich and
influential, rising from one office to another, from
being head of his department to be governor of a village, and then of more villages, of towns, or of nomes,
until he became almost second to the Pharaoh himself.
Such was the history of the scribe Amten, who lived
under King Sneferu of the IVth Dynasty, and whose
tomb, discovered near Abusîr, was removed to Berlin.

Scribes figure on every tomb wall, for the Egyptians seem to have been extremely methodical in
every detail of management, and to have been slaves
to red tape. One man writes to another on a matter
of business, and says, "I write this to you that it
may serve as a witness between us, and you must
keep this letter, that in future it may serve as a
witness." Thoth was the god specially prayed to by
scribes, he being the inventor of writing.

The scribes represented the culture and intelligence
of the kingdom. In the processions of the gods the
" chief of the scribes " took precedence of the high
priest of Åmen. The " royal scribe " appears to have
been a most important functionary, and princes of the
XVIIIth and XIXth Dynasties have been found to
bear this title. Women were admitted to the rank of
scribes.

Seb or Qeb. The earth personified as a god. He

was the son of Shu, the husband of
Nut, the sky, and father of Osiris, Set,
Isis, and Nephthys. His symbol is a
goose, and he is represented in human
form with that bird upon his head.
He is called "the great cackler," and
by some was supposed to have laid the
egg from which the earth and all
things sprang. In the later texts "the
back of Seb" is a common name for
the earth.

Seb.

Sebek. A god represented either as
a crocodile, or as human with the head
of a crocodile. He seems to have
played various rôles, one especially as an evil deity
in antagonism to the other deities,
and as such at times confused with Set.
The double temple at Kom Ombo was
partly dedicated to his cult, and the
Fayûm was also a great centre of his
worship. That he was one of the
oldest gods of the Egyptian Pantheon
is evidenced by the fact that his name
has been incorporated into many royal
names of the XIIIth Dynasty. The
sacred lake of the temple to Sebek in
the Fayûm contained numbers of the
sacred crocodiles, which, according to
Strabo, were decorated with jewels and
fed by the priests. Sukhos is the Greek
name of the god.

Sebek.

Sebek-em-saf I., *Rā-sekhem-uaz-khāu.* Probably a

XIIIth Dynasty king. His name is found at Ham-
māmāt, and a statue and statuette have been found
bearing his name.

Sebek-em-sauf II., *Rā-sekhem-s-shedi-taui.* This

king is only known to us from the Abbott and
Amherst papyri. His queen was Nub-khā-s he
appears to have had three children.

Sebek-hetep I, *Rā-sekhem-khu.*

Sebek-hetep II., *Rā-sekhem-suaz-taui.* Two kings

of Dynasty XIII., cir. 2420 B.C., whose names are of
frequent occurrence, but of whom little is known at
present.

Sebek-hetep III., *Rā-khā-nefer.* A king of

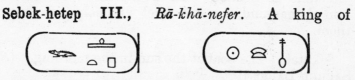

Dynasty XIII. There are more monumental remains
of this king than of any other of this dynasty.

Sebek-neferu (Queen).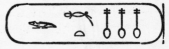

Eighth and last monarch of Dynasty XII, circa
2569 B.C. She was the daughter of Åmen-em-hāt III.
and sister of Åmen-em-hāt IV.

Sebennythos. Greek name for *Theb-netert*, capital
of the twelfth nome of Lower Egypt, the modern
Samanhûd. The chief deity was Ånher.

Seker. *See* PTAH-SEKER-OSIRIS.

Seker-nefer-ka. Eighth king of Dynasty II. According to tradition this king was a giant, being 5 cubits 3 palms in height, or just over 8 ft.

Sekhem. The most sacred place in an Egyptian temple, in which was placed the shrine containing the emblem of the titular deity.

Sekhet.

Sekhet. A goddess, second person of the triad at Memphis, who was considered to be the wife of Ptah and mother of Nefer Tum and Im-ḥetep. She is represented with a lioness' head with the disk and uraeus. Like the other lioness- or cat-headed deities, she represented the power of the sun. But Sekhet must have represented its great heat, for a text at Philae says of Isis that she is " terrible as Sekhet." In the legend of the destruction of mankind, it was Sekhet who helped to destroy them.

Sekhtet. The boat of the sun in the morning. (*See* SACRED BARKS.)

Selk or Serqet. A goddess of like nature with Isis, also a protectress of the canopic jars. She is figured with a scorpion on the top of her head, or sometimes as a scorpion with a human head. She was a daughter of Rā, is at times identified with Safekh, and perhaps symbolized the scorching heat of the sun.

Selk.

Semneh. A crude brick fort still standing on the west bank of the Nile, erected by Usertsen III. for the protection of his southern frontier from the raids of the Nubians. It stands on an artificial platform of commanding height. (*See* KUMMEH.)

Sen-mut. *See* ARCHITECTS.

Senta. Fifth king of Dynasty II. Reigned forty-one (?) years. This king is mentioned in the Berlin Medical Papyrus; and on the tomb of Shery, a priest.

Se-qenen-Rā I., *Ta-āa*, Dynasty XVII., cir. 1660 B.C.

the queen of this king was Āāh-ḥetep, and we know of two sons, one of whom died young, and one daughter. Nothing is known about this king except that his was one of the royal tombs inspected under the Rames-sides.

Seqenen-Rā III., *Ta-āa-qen*, Dynasty XVII., cir.

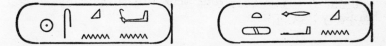

1610, B.C. Āāh-ḥetep was his queen, and he had several children; the celebrated Princess Nefert-àri being one of them. The coffin containing the king's mummy was found among the "Royal find" at Dêr el Baḥri in 1881. Evidently he had fallen on the battle-field and died of his wounds. Petrie suggests that he was a Berberi.

It was for Queen Āāh-ḥetep that the magnificent jewellery, found buried with her a few feet under the sand at Dra-abu'l-Negga, was made. It is now in the Cairo Museum.

Serapēum. This name is incorrectly given to the Apis mausoleum at Sakkâra. The Serapēum proper was the temple built over the site of the excavated tombs, of which the very few remains are covered with sand. The ruins were discovered by Mariette in 1860. The word is a combination of the two Egyptian words —Osiris-Apis, a combination of which the Greeks made their god Serāpis (*q.v.*). The huge vaults opened by Mariette consist of three parts, one which originally contained the bulls of the period from Ámen-ḥetep III. to the XXth Dynasty, another those of XXIInd to XXVth Dynasties, and the third part those from the reign of Psammetichus I. (XXVIth Dynasty) to the time of the later Ptolemies. Thus the burials cover a period of about 1450 years, i.e. from about 1500 B.C. to 50 B.C.

Only the third part is open to the public, the two first being covered with sand. This part consists of one long gallery excavated in the rock, and some shorter ones. On either side of the long gallery are deep pits in which are the enormous sarcophagi. These are monoliths of red or black granite, or limestone, the average measurements being—length, 13 ft., width, 8 ft., height, 11 ft. Mariette found the covers of most of the sarcophagi pushed aside and the contents gone. Of the twenty-four that are there, only three bore any inscription.

The **Serapēum** or **Serapeion** at Alexandria was a temple of Serāpis founded by Ptolemy Soter, which was said to be only surpassed in splendour by the Capitol at Rome. It was destroyed by order of Theo-dosius in A.D. 389.

Serāpis, i.e. **Osiris-Apis,** or **Áusár Hāpi.** This god is a combination of the Apis with Osiris, and was introduced into Egypt by the Ptolemies. He is accounted to be the second son of Ptah, and is represented with a bull's head surmounted by a disk and uraeus. His worship extended all over the kingdom, and was very popular under the Roman domination.

Serdāb. A hidden chamber or cell in the tomb; from an Arabic word for a "hidden" chamber. In the Serdāb were deposited *Ka* statues (*q.v.*) of the deceased. Usually it was completely sealed up, but sometimes a small aperture was left communicating with the tomb chapel, through which incense or perfume might reach the statues. The walls of Serdābs were not decorated.

Serpents. As with all early civilizations the cult of serpents enters largely into Egyptian religion. Large numbers of them appear on tomb walls, some of evil portent, but perhaps as many of good. They were enemies of the sun-god, opposing his progress during his journey through the underworld through the twelve hours of night, and as such Bes and Ta-urt are their foes, and are often seen strangling them. In the tomb of Seti I., at Thebes, many scenes with serpents are depicted. In one the ithyphallic god, Nehebka, in the form of a serpent with arms and legs, opposes the progress of the solar bark in which is Horus standing upon a winged snake. The chief of all the evil serpents was Ápepi or Apophis (*q.v.*), who seems to have been a personification of spiritual evil. There is a religious work called the "Book of the Overthrowing of Ápepi" (*q.v.*). A spirit of fear and the idea of propitiation probably led to the great popularity to which this cult at one time attained.

Three kinds of serpents are represented on the monuments. (*a*) The *cobra di capello* (*uraeus*)—the *basilisk* of the Greeks, which was the symbol of divine and royal sovereignty, and is seen on the forehead of gods and kings. (*b*) The *asp* or *cerastes*, a poisonous viper, possibly the "cockatrice" of Scripture. (*c*) A great *coluber* of what species not yet determined. It was this last that represented the Typhonian Ápepi.

Many magical formulae against snakes have been found.

Servants. There is a word in the inscriptions which has been translated " slave," but it is not impossible that it means servant more in our modern sense. Slaves in the real sense of the word were importations, having either been bought from some foreign merchant, or been captured in war. They were the actual property of their masters, serfs attached to the soil; but there is no good evidence that they were cruelly treated. There must have been great numbers in Egypt, for we find that " in thirty years Ramses III. presented 113,433 of them to the temples alone. The ' Directors of the Royal Slaves ' at all periods, occupied an important position at the court of the Pharaohs."

Then, as now, a man's importance was partly measured by the number of servants he kept. A high official under Usertsen I. of the XIIth Dynasty had sixty-three officers and servants enumerated on the walls of his tomb at Beni Hasan. Of these there were nine " food providers," five scribes, seven maid house-messengers, a superintendent of canals, four herdsmen, and nine priests. Among the chief servants were those who had to do with food-providing. In the tombs at Tel el Amarna we find among other servants the following : " Superintendent of the provision house, superintendent of the dwelling, superintendent of the bakehouse, scribe of the libations, bearer of cool drinks, preparer of sweets."

Seshta. The goddess of learning ; her name is often, but incorrectly, written Safekh (*q.v.*).

Sesostris. (*See* RAMSES II.)

Set. The god whom the Greeks identified with their Typhon. He was the son of Nut and Seb, born of Nut on the third of the epagomenal days (*q.v.*), hence brother to Osiris. His wife is Nephthys

Mention of him is made in the oldest texts, and in these
early times his offices were bene-
ficent, and he is spoken of with as
much reverence as the other gods.
He was not originally a god of evil,
but as personifying natural darkness
he gradually came to be so regarded. His victory (as representing night) over his brother Osiris,
who, as the sun, sank in the west
at the end of his day's journey, was
looked on in later times as an
aggressive warfare. In the time of
the decline of the empire he was
regarded with abhorrence, and his
name erased from the monuments;
but the very fact that his name
formed part of some royal names
shows that this detestation was a
later development. The district about Kom Ombos
was at one time a centre of his cult, and at Tanis he
also seems to have been held in special reverence. He
is represented with a human body, and the head of
an animal which has not yet been identified.

Set.

Seten ḥetep tā. The commencement of the universal
formula found in tombs which constitutes a kind of
prayer for benefits for the deceased. It has been
translated in many different ways, none of which are
entirely satisfactory. "A royal oblation give," &c.
"A royal table of propitiation grant," &c. The whole
prayer runs on these lines: "A royal oblation grant
Osiris, dwelling in Amenti, Lord of Abydos. May he
grant the funeral oblations, bread, beer, oxen, geese,
wine, milk, oil, incense, wrappings, all gifts of vegeta-
tion, whatever heaven gives, or earth produces, to
enjoy the Nile, to come forth as a living soul, that the
soul may not be repulsed at the gates of the nether
world, to be glorified among the favoured ones in
presence of Un-nefer, to breathe the delicious breezes

of the north wind, and to drink from the depth of the river." About the time of the XIIth Dynasty and onwards this prayer is distinctly for the *Ka* (*q.v.*) of the deceased.

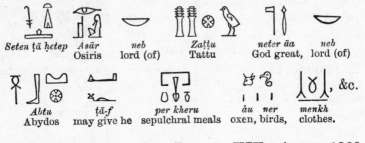

Seten ṭā ḥetep — *A sār* Osiris — *neb* lord (of) — *Zaṭṭu* Tattu — *neter āa* God great, — *neb* lord (of)

Abtu Abydos — *ṭā-f* may give he — *per kheru* sepulchral meals — *āu ner* oxen, birds, — *menkh* clothes. &c.

Seti I. *Maāt-men-Rā.* Dynasty XIX., cir. B.C. 1366

The early years of this king's reign were troubled by the constant incursions of the tribes from the neighbourhood of the Delta, and on the walls of the temple of Karnak may be seen a vivid representation of the principal events of the successful campaign against the Shasu. Having been victorious in the Delta, Seti I. pushed on to Kadesh on the Orontes to punish Mauthanar the Kheta king, who had broken the treaty made between himself and Ramses I. After this we find the Pharaoh waging war against the Libyans, and the Cushites in the south. The temples of Abydos and Gurnah, and the Great Hall of Columns at Karnak are among the most lasting memorials of this king's fame; and his tomb in the Biban el Molouk is the largest of the celebrated rock-cut burial places. The mother of his son and successor, Ramses II., was Tiu, a granddaughter of Khu-en-aten. The mummy of Seti I. is in the Cairo Museum.

Sethroë. Greek name of the capital of one of the nomes of Lower Egypt, which has not yet been identified. De Rougé thinks it must have been in the fourteenth, *Khent-abt*. It may be *Thekut*. The chief deity was Atmu.

Setna, the papyrus of, in the Cairo Museum, written in the second or third century B.C., was found at Thebes with some other manuscripts, in a wooden box, which was taken from the tomb of a Coptic monk, and probably constituted the library of this Egyptian. Though, unlike the " Tale of Two Brothers," it is written in demotic, the style of it is very similar to that of the earlier papyrus, the grammar being, Brugsch says, quite the same. The colophon, which does not give the author's name, reads thus : " This is the end of the manuscript which tells the story of Setna Kharmes, and of Ptahneferka, and of Ahura his wife, and of Merhu his son, written in the year 35, the . . . day of the month Tybi ; " that is the thirty-fifth year of one of the Ptolemies. Setna is twice called " the son of the king User-maāt," that is Ramses II. The story tells of a search for the sacred book of Thoth, and of the calamities its possession brought on the finders. (*See* " Records of Past," vi., p. 131, translated by Goodwin ; also translations into French by Maspero and into English by Griffith ; Brugsch, in " Revue Archéologique," Septembre, 1867 ; M. Soury, in " Revue des Deux Mondes," February 15th, 1875.)

Shabaka, *Sabaco*, or *So*. 2 Kings, xvii. 4. King of Ethiopia, B.C. 700, Dynasty XXV.

Shadoof. The ordinary shadoof, such as that still used in the country, was the usual means employed in ancient Egypt for lifting water from the Nile. It consists of a pole resting on an upright post, or on a horizontal beam supported on two columns of brick or mud, having at one end a weight which serves as a counterpoise to the bucket.

Shai. The god of destiny, associated with Renenet, goddess of fortune. He decreed what should happen to men. He figures with Renenet and Meskhent in the scenes of the weighing of the heart in the judgment hall of Osiris. His name signifies to divide or portion out. (*See* PSYCHOSTASIA.)

Shashanq. *See* SHISHAK.

Shasu. A tribe inhabiting the deserts of north Arabia and Syria, with whom the kings of Egypt were perpetually in conflict—literally, Bedawin. Thus their name figures among those of conquered peoples on temple walls in inscriptions of Thothmes II., Amenhetep II., Amen-hetep IV., Seti I., and Ramses II. In campaigns carried on in Syria it was inevitable that the marching Egyptian armies should come into collision with these people, since they were obliged to pass through their territory.

Shenthit. Funeral form of Isis. At Busiris, Abydos, and Dendera were sanctuaries dedicated to her.

Shepherd Kings. *See* HYKSOS.

Shepses-ka-f.  Sixth king of

Dynasty IV., cir. 3759 B.C. Reigned twenty-two years. From the tomb of Ptah-Shepses, at Sakkâra, we learn that his eldest daughter was Maāt-khā.

Shishak I. Dynasty XXII., cir. B.C. 966.

This king is chiefly known as the monarch to whose court Jeroboam fled (1 Kings xi. 26-40). In the fifth year of Rehoboam's reign, and possibly at the instigation of Jeroboam, Shishak marched against Judah and pillaged Jerusalem (1 Kings xiv. 25-28; 2 Chron. xii.). Among the names of the conquered Syrian districts and towns engraved upon the walls of the temple of Karnak is that of Judah-melek, which some have considered represents the *king* or *kingdom of Judah*. Maspero, on the other hand, believes that it is more likely to be Jehudah, a town of the tribe of Dan.

Shrew-mice. These little creatures were sometimes mummified, and have been found in small bronze cases with a figure of the mouse on the top. It was sacred to Her-khent-an-ma, a form of Horus, supposed to be blind, who was worshipped in Letopolis.

Shu. The son of Rā and Hathor, though a later legend says that Rā produced Shu and Tefnut (*q.v.*) without the co-operation of a goddess. As a nature god he may be said to be a personification of the atmosphere which divides the sky (Nut) from the earth (Seb). He is frequently figured with arms uplifted, supporting the starry Nut, while Seb lies beneath. He is represented as a man, with his symbol the feather on the top of his head. The little faïence figures of Shu holding up the sun-disk, represent the god placing the sun in its right position between sky and earth. He is the twin-brother of Tefnut, the two being frequently associated as two lions.

Shu.

Silver. From old inscriptions it is clear that silver was looked upon as the most precious metal, possibly because there was not any found in Egypt. Under the New Empire, when gold and electron came more into use, it decreased very much in value.

Silver was imported into Egypt from Asia in rings, bricks, and sheets of standard weight. It was called in the hieroglyphs " white gold," from which it is inferred that gold was known to the Egyptians prioi to silver. Few objects made in this metal remain, among them are specimens of statuettes, some chains and rings, and a few vases—part of a temple treasure.

Silver was sometimes used for making the eyes of statuettes.

Sistrum. A musical instrument, formed of a loop of bronze ribbon fastened to a handle, crossed by three or four metal bars passing through holes in each side of the loop. These bars were quite loose, being merely bent at each end to keep them from slipping out, and they sometimes bore metal rings, which considerably added to the sound when the instrument was shaken. Sometimes the bars were in the form of little serpents. The sistrum was one of the usual attributes of the goddess Hathor, and was used as a design for the capitals of columns over the head of Hathor. The handles of the instruments were almost always in the form of the head of that goddess, and were usually of bronze, sometimes inlaid with silver. Enamelled handles have also been found. The length of the whole varied from eight to sixteen or eighteen inches. Plutarch mentions (*de Iside*, s. 63) that the sistrum was supposed by some to have the power of frightening away Typhon, or the evil spirit. Sistra were used in the most solemn religious services, when they were often carried by women of high rank. Models of sistra in enamelled ware were often deposited in the tombs, but were first broken in sign of mourning. (*See* Brit. Mus., 4th Egyptian Room, table case A.)

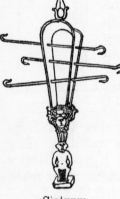

Sistrum.

Sivan. *See* NEKHEBT.

Slaves. *See* SERVANTS.

Sneferu. First king of Dynasty IV., cir. 3998 B.C., reigned twenty-nine years. Two queens are known, Mertitefs and

Meri-s-ankh, and one daughter, Nefert-kau. The pyramid and temple at Medûm belong to this king. From the Sinai tablet it is evident that Sneferu sent an expedition against the Bedawi. (*See* MEDÛM.)

Sokaris, or **Sokar**, or **Seker**. A god of whom little is known except when in combination with others. He was a sun-god at one time, and his emblem was carried round at festivals in the sacred bark called *hennu*. The great festival of Sokaris was held at Memphis, in connection with the winter solstice. To him, it seems, especially belonged the fourth and fifth hours of the night, through which Râ, the sun, nightly passed during his journey from sunset to dawn. He is represented as a mummy with a hawk's head. (*See* PTAH-SEKER-OSIRIS.)

Sopt, or **Sepd**, the god of the Arabian nome, and, according to Wiedemann, some-times identified with Bes (*q.v.*). He is described upon the monu-ments at Saft el-Henneh as " Sopt, the Spirit of the East, the Hawk, the Horus of the East," and as connected with Tum (*q.v.*). Naville considers him to be the herald of the sun. He probably represents the zodiacal light, the long pyramidal shaft of light seen after the sun has set or before he rises. The fact that his symbol is a high, narrow pyramid con-firms this supposition.

Sopt.

Sothis. The Greek form of the Egyptian word for Sirius, the brilliant star in the constellation Canis, from whence its name the dog-star, perhaps the most important star known to Egyptian astronomers. Its importance also to the modern chronologer can hardly be over-estimated, for the Egyptian calendar was arranged by the heliacal rising of Sothis. The star was personified as a goddess, and frequently represented, especially in the Graeco-Roman temples, as a cow. She is queen of the thirty-six constellations recorded in old astronomical tables, and was the star of Isis. Part of the temple at Dendera was devoted to the festivals in honour of the rising of Sothis. (*See* YEAR.)

Soul. *See* BA and KA.

Speos. A Greek word used to designate a small rock-cut temple or shrine.

Speos Artemidos. The Greek name given to a small rock-cut temple at *Beni Hasan*. It was begun by Queen Hatshepsut and Thothmes III. of the XVIIIth Dynasty. It is dedicated to Bast, one of the lioness-headed goddesses, whom the Greeks identified with their Artemis—the Roman Diana.

Sphinx. The oldest known monument in Egypt, standing on the Gîzeh platform about a quarter of a mile S.E. of the great pyramid. Its date is unknown; but an inscription of Khufu mentions it, and possibly it was restored by this king; though some Egyptologists consider that it is of much later date. It is hewn out of the solid rock, the deficiency in contour being supplied by masonry. The body is about 150 ft. long, the paws 50 ft., the greatest height about 70 ft., the head being 30 ft. long, and the breadth of face 14 ft. The features have been spoiled by Mohammedan fanaticism that made a target of the face. But some of the original red colouring still remains on the cheek. Parts of the beard and uraeus are now in the British Museum [N. Egyptian Gallery]. More than once the monument has been cleared from the sand which constantly drifts round to and buries it. Of late years the Egyptian Government has made extensive excavations here.

Between the paws of the Sphinx, Thothmes IV. set up a tablet recording the appearance to him of Harmachis in an after-dinner sleep, when he was promised great rewards by the god if he would dig the Sphinx—his image—out of the sand. In Egyptian its name is ⫯ 𓅃 𓄿 " hu," and it represented "Horus on the horizon"—Heru-em-khut, better known as Harmachis.

Sports. Representations of various games and pastimes occur on the tomb walls. Hunting and fishing were favourite pursuits. Gazelles and antelopes, even lions were hunted in the desert with the aid of hounds. Lassoes and bow and arrows were used. Fishing as an amusement was practised with a line and hook, or the sportsman went into the marshes in a light skiff and speared the fish with a bident. Mock fights in small boats and war-dances were indulged in. Bird-snaring was also a favourite pursuit. Many kinds of traps and nets are depicted on the tomb-walls, several for catching one bird at a time, and one very large one. This latter measured about 10 ft. by 5 ft., and was made of netted string on a frame ; but the construction and method of working are difficult to understand. Wrestling, with closed or open hand, was a military exercise for rendering the body supple. Scenes showing men thus engaged occur in long sequences in the tombs at Beni Hasan. At large entertainments and feasts, of which they seemed to be very fond, the guests were amused by dancing women and music (*see* DANCE and MUSIC); also by men and women who performed acrobatic feats, or were skilful at throwing the ball. Tomb-pictures show women swinging one another round by the arms, bending back until the head nearly touches the heels, and so on. (*See* GAMES.)

Stela, or Stele. Egyptian stelae are of all sizes, from small portable slabs like miniature tombstones to the great slab of black syenite, 10 ft. 3 ins. high, called the Israel Stela (*q.v.*). They have been found in a variety of materials—granite, limestone, wood, and pottery. The majority are sepulchral, bearing inscriptions relating to the life of the deceased, his titles and relatives. They contain also forms of prayers. These stelae were placed in the tomb in various positions. The earliest examples are square at the top, the later ones rounded. The latter are frequently decorated at the top with the disk and wings. In the early dynasties they usually bear pictures of the deceased, accompanied by his wife and family, and are often coloured, while in the time of the XVIIIth Dynasty the relatives gave place to representations of gods. The biographies on these stelae have been of the greatest importance to chronologers and historians, and in some cases are the only authorities for certain periods.

Stelae, other than sepulchral, are inscribed with records of important events in certain reigns, decrees, religious hymns, &c. Sometimes these are given in two or three languages, which renders the tablet of great value. Such are the Rosetta Stone (*q.v.*), and one found at Philae in hieroglyphs, Greek, and Latin.

Stibium. A cosmetic in frequent use for painting the eyes. The best kind is known in the hieroglyphs under the name of *meszemt*. Besides being used for purposes of adornment, it was probably used for the eyes in cases of ophthalmia, on account of its healing properties, that disease being frequent in ancient times.

Strabo. The famous Greek geographer of the first century B.C. In the year 24 B.C. he visited Egypt, and ascended the Nile as far as Syene and Philae with the prefect Aelius Gallus. He then spent some years in Alexandria, which was then the great world-centre of learning, amassing materials for his great work. This geography is the most important work on the subject that has come down to us from classic times. It is in the last (XVIIth) book of his geography that he describes Egypt, Ethiopia, and the north coast of Libya.

Stream, The Great. Understood by Renouf to mean the Milky Way; here, according to the " Book of the Dead," purification was obtained.

Sun. The sun was personified under the form of Rä (*q.v.*). Many of his attributes, and different aspects were also personified. Osiris was the night sun, Tum the setting sun, Horus at times the rising sun. The lioness- and cat-headed goddesses represent varying degrees of the heat of the sun. The Egyptian conception of the sky being that it was a vast ocean, they represented the sun disk sailing across this in a bark.

Sutekh. A name given to SET (*q.v.*).

Sycomore. The *persea* and *sycomore* trees were the most important of the sacred trees of Egypt. It was sacred to Nut and Hathor, whose doubles were supposed to inhabit it. The " Sycomore of the South " was regarded as " the living body of Hathor on earth," the Memphite Hathor being called " Lady of the Southern Sycomore." The peasants made offerings of fruits and vegetables and water in jars to such trees, as may be seen from pictures in the tombs. The " Land of the Sycomore " was a name given to the Memphite and Letopolite nomes. The tree is the wild fig. (*See* TREES, SACRED.)

Syene. The Scriptural name for Aswân. It gives its name to a particular form of granite found there and hence called syenite. The name is derived from the hieroglyphic *sun*. It owed its ancient importance to its granite quarries, whence material for temples, obelisks, and statues was taken, and on account of its being a frontier town between Egypt proper and

Nubia. In Ptolemaic times it was considered to lie immediately under the tropic, because it was noticed that during the summer solstice the rays of the sun fell vertically to the bottom of a well in the town. This well has not been discovered. Eratosthenes made use of this fact in his calculations for the measurement of the earth.

Syenite. *See* GRANITE.

T

Taharqa, *Tirhakah* (2 Kings xix. 9), king of Ethiopia. Dynasty XXV., B.C. 693. He is best known to history for having rescued Hezekiah, king of Judah, out of the hands of Sennacherib, king of Assyria, whom he conquered. Later on Taharqa was in turn defeated by the son and grandson of the Assyrian king.

Tahpanhes, the Greek **Daphnae,** the present **Tell Defenneh.** The ruins of an old frontier fortress and camp known as "The Palace of the Jew's Daughter." Probably the original garrison of the Carian and Ionian mercenaries by whose aid Psammetichus I. fought his way to the throne of Egypt, and whose foundation deposits were discovered beneath the four corners of the fort (Herod. ii. 30 and ii. 154). It was the home of Zedekiah's daughters after Jerusalem had been besieged and taken by Nebuchadnezzar, king of Babylon, B.C. 588 (Jer. xliii. 6, 7; Josephus, Ant. ix. 7). In the reign of Amāsis (Āāḥmes II.) the whole Greek garrison was deported to Memphis and its place taken by Egyptians, who in their turn were succeeded by a Persian garrison.

Tanen. An earth god, another form of Seb (*q.v.*). He is also combined with Ptah, the god Ptah-Tanen being more often spoken of than Tanen alone. At Abu Simbel he is described as father to Ramses II. He is represented as a man with the ram's horns, two feathers and disk on his head. Tanen, besides being a personification of the earth, is also identified with the night sun. He is the presiding deity of the land bordering on Lake Moeris.

Tanis. The Greek name for *Zānt*, the capital of the fourteenth nome of Lower Egypt, the modern Sān, and Scriptural Zoan. Chief deity, Horus.

Taricheutes. An embalmer of the dead.

Ta-urt, or Thoueris. The goddess represented as a hippopotamus, though occasionally with a woman's head, and sometimes as a whole woman. She was the wife of Set, and was supposed by some at Thebes, where she was worshipped as **Apet**, to have given birth to Osiris. Her head-dress is usually the disk, horns and plumes,

and she is shown leaning on the ⚱

Ta-urt.

the amulet which represented the blood of Isis. She is called " mistress of the gods," also the " good nurse," for she presided at the birth of children.

Taxation. It is evident from various records that there was a regular system of taxation, and that in old days even as now the people only paid under protest. There is no evidence of a poll tax even as late as the time of the early Ptolemies. But when at regular intervals several times a year the tax-collector came, each village would be a scene of distress and uproar until each debtor had paid up his due, probably only induced to do so by the stick. In Ptolemaic times there was an elaborate and crushing system of taxation, the injustice arising probably from the fact that the collection of the taxes was farmed out. Ptolemy V. instituted a five per cent. tax on all sales.

Tefnut.

Tefnut, twin sister to SHU and daughter of Rā and Hathor. As a nature goddess she probably represents the dew. Philae, Elephantiné, Memphis, Dendera, &c., were centres of her cult, but the conceptions of her functions varied. She is represented with a lion's head, with the disk and uraeus above. In the pyramid texts she is supposed to carry away thirst from the deceased.

Tel el Amarna. The name of the modern village which marks the site of *Khut-Áten* (*q.v.*).

Tel-el-Amarna Tablets. East of the Royal palace of Khu-en-Áten (*q.v.*) or Akht-Áten was discovered the "House of the Royal Rolls." One of the most important archaeological finds of modern times was made here in 1887, in the shape of three hundred clay tablets inscribed in the cuneiform character. They proved to be despatches and letters from the neighbouring kings of Babylon, Assyria, Mitanni, and Cappadocia, also from the Egyptian rulers in Jerusalem, Canaan, the "field of Bashan," and Syria. They throw a great deal of light, not only on the history of the reign of Atch-en-Áten, but on the state of Palestine, and the relations existing between the powers at that time. Among the letter writers are Burnaburyas, king of Babylonia, Dushratta, king of Mitanni, and Ebed-tob, the vassal king of Jerusalem. (*See* ÁMEN-HETEP IV.)

Temple. The Egyptian temple was not built as are Christian churches or Mohammedan mosques, for the purposes of public worship and instruction; its very arrangement at once precludes such possibilities. It was generally erected by a monarch as a shrine for the tutelary deity first, and then as the personal monument raised by him to himself, on which may be seen his deeds of prowess, the slaughter of his enemies, his dedication of gifts to the presiding deity, &c.

The earliest temples were evidently of wood or wattle, and were merely the shrines enclosing the symbols of the god; under the Old Empire they were built of stone, i.e. temples of the Second Pyramid at Gîzeh, and of King Sneferu at Medûm, but were severely simple; under the New Empire the temple became much more complicated, from the fact that successive kings enlarged their predecessors' buildings by adding halls of columns, chambers, &c. The essential plan of every temple was practically the same—a crude brick surrounding wall, the pylon or entrance gateway, with flanking towers, before which generally stood two colossal statues of the king and two obelisks, and the naos, containing the innermost sanctuary where was kept the divine symbol. In course of time this simple plan became expanded into a most complicated structure, reached sometimes by as many as three pylons, separated by three avenues of sphinxes, and followed by columned courts, a hypostyle or columnar hall, and flanked by numerous chambers, where the books, vestments, and treasures of the temple were kept; all of which led up to the *sekhem* or holy place. The roof was always constructed of flat slabs of stone, while light has admitted either by stone gratings or by small shafts in the roofing slabs.

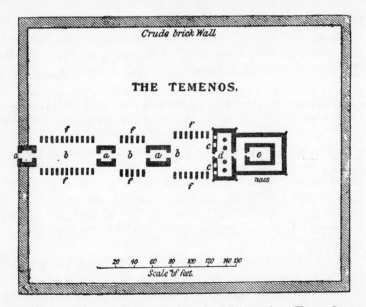

Plan of very simple form of an Egyptian Temple:—
a, the Pylons; *b*, the Dromos flanked by Sphinxes *f*;
c, screen; *d*, the Pro-naos; *e*, the Adytum—which in
this example is within the Naos. In some cases the
Adytum or sanctuary fills the whole of the Naos.

Tenait. One of the feasts commemorative and repre-
sentative of the death of Osiris, held on the seventh day
of the month. In the great text from the temple of Dendera there are directions for its celebration. Tenait is
also the name of the fifth hour of the day and of certain
days in the month.

Tentyris. The Greek name for Ta-en-tarert, capital
of the sixth nome of Upper Egypt, the modern Dendera. Chief deity, Hathor.

Tesherit. The "red land," or region of the Arabian
desert.

Tetâ I. First king of Dynasty

His pyramid, *Dad-asut*, at Sakkâra, exists in a ruined condition.

Tetâ II. The second king of Dynasty I. Reigned fifty-seven years. He is said to have continued the buildings at Memphis that were begun by his father, Mena; tradition also assigns some medical works to him.

Tetâ III. Sixth king of Dynasty III. Reigned nineteen (?) years.

Thebaïd. The great district of which Thebes was the capital. Its northern frontier was at Thebaïca Phylakè, which was a fortified place where duty was levied on goods going north. The site is probably at the modern Darut-el-Sherif.

Thigh, The, Egyptian *Khepersh.* The iron instrument used by the priests in the ceremony of opening the mouth of the deceased. The constellation of the Great Bear was also called the Thigh.

This or Thinis. One of the most ancient towns in Egypt, the exact site of which has not been discovered. It was the metropolis of the eighth nome of Upper Egypt, and must have lain in the district between Abydos and the modern Girgeh. The Ist Dynasty of Egyptian kings, called Thinite, was said to have come from there. MENÀ, the first king of Egypt, was a Thinite. It is only from this fact that the place is of any importance, it having otherwise but a mean existence. A stela of the XIIth Dynasty shows that the oasis of Dakhel came under a prince of This called Àntef. (*See* ÀNHUR.)

Thoth or Tehuti. One of the principal gods of Egypt, whose cult was less confined to one particular district than that of almost any other god. His name signifies "the measurer," and as such he is a lunar

Thoth.

deity and wears the lunar crescent and disk. Two animals are especially sacred to him, the ibis and the cynocephalus. Sometimes the god is represented as an ibis, but most frequently he appears in human form with the head of that bird surmounted by the crescent and disk, and carrying either a palette and pen, or the notched palm branch. He is always found in the judgment scenes, where he records on his palette the result of the weighing of the heart of the deceased. He was the inventor of all the exact sciences, letters, learning and the fine arts. He wrote the sacred books and had as great knowledge of magic as Isis. The Greeks identified him with Hermes. (*See* HERMES TRISMEGISTOS.)

Thothmes I., *Āa-kheper-ka-Rā*, Dynasty XVIII., cir.

B.C. 1541—1516. It is from the tombs of the two Court officials, Áāhmes and Pen-nekheb, at El-Kab, that we learn that this king subdued the Nubians, the "Anu of Khent," and the people of Upper Mesopotamia, as far as the city of Niy, situated near Aleppo and on the Euphrates.

Thothmes I. married Áāhmes and Mut-nefert, and had three children. He was succeeded by his son, Thothmes II. His mummy is in the Cairo Museum.

Thothmes II., *Āah-kheper-en-Rā*, Dynasty XVIII.,

B.C. 1516—1503. Married his half sister, Ḥātshepsut

and Åset, not of royal blood, by whom he had three children. His only son, Thothmes III., was his successor. Perhaps it was owing to his delicate health that this king seems to have left the government of the country chiefly in the hands of Queen Ḥātshepsut. He appears to have maintained his predecessor's authority in Cush, in "the land of the Fenkhu" (Phoenicians), and round the shores of the Mediterranean. His mummy is in the Cairo Museum.

Thothmes III., *Men-kheper-Rā*, Dynasty XVIII.,

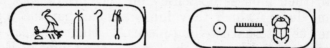

cir. B.C. 1503—1449. His two queens are Meryt-Rā Ḥātshepset, his cousin, and Nebtu. He had one son, who succeeded him, and several daughters. The actual pedigree of this king has for long been a matter of doubt. That he was the son of Åset, who was a concubine and not a queen, is absolutely certain, but whether he was the son of Thothmes I. or II. has been under grave discussion, and Egyptologists are not yet unanimous upon the point. Probably he was the son of Thothmes II.

Thothmes IV., *Men-kheperu-Rā*, Dynasty XVIII.,

cir. B.C. 1423—1414. He married Mut-em-ua, and had two sons, one of whom, Åmen-hetep III., succeeded him. He asserted the power of Egypt in Nubia and Syria, but is better known from the reference to himself upon the stela between the paws of the Sphinx. On this the king relates how, in consequence of a dream, he removed the sands of the desert which was spoiling the image of the god.

Tin. Very little tin has been discovered in Egypt,

and no word for it in the hieroglyphs has yet been
found No traces have yet appeared of the sources
whence the tin used in making bronze was obtained.
Objects in pure tin are extremely rare. Professor Petrie
discovered a pure tin ring set with glass at Gurob.
(*See* BRONZE.)

Tomb. Egypt is a land of tombs. Yet with all the
care bestowed on the tomb, but little remains of any
houses of the Egyptians. This fact is easily accounted
for if Diodorus is correct in saying, " The Egyptians
call their houses hostelries, on account of the short
time during which they inhabit them, but the tombs
they call eternal dwelling-places." Hence the elabora-
tion in every detail of the tomb. The tombs of Egypt
fall naturally into two classes—those excavated in the
rock and those which were built. Of the former kind
there are examples covering the entire historic period.
The latter belong to the time of the early dynasties.
They are of two kinds, pyramids and mastăbas (*q.v.*).
The great groups of rock-cut tombs are those of the
VIth and other dynasties at Aswân, those of the XIIth
Dynasty at Beni Hasan, those of the XVIIIth and
successive dynasties of Pharaohs at Thebes ; those of
Khu-en-aten and his people at Tel-el-Amarna. But
besides these main groups there are tombs in almost
every available hillside throughout the country. The
idea in the construction of all these tombs was essen-
tially the same, though carried out in different ways.
Each consisted of three parts—(*a*) a chamber or series
of chambers forming a kind of chapel, (*b*) a passage or
shaft, leading to (*c*) the sepulchral chamber. The
tomb was prepared during the lifetime of the man.
The scenes with which the walls of the chambers were
decorated represented in the majority of cases the occu-
pations of its owner. If, for instance, he was an admiral,
we find pictures of ships and the spoil brought from
foreign lands. There are fishing and fowling scenes,
representations of the chase, and other amusements.
In a secret chamber (Serdāb, *q.v.*) in the wall were

placed the Ka statues, a small aperture sometimes being left by which the smoke of incense might penetrate to the statues.

In the case of rock-cut tombs the sepulchral chamber was reached by a deep shaft (the deepest known is that in the tomb of Bakt III. at Beni Hasan; it is over 105 ft.) which, after the body was deposited, was filled up with rubble, the great object being to secure the mummy from disturbance.

The scenes on the chamber walls are sometimes in low relief, at others only painted, the accompanying hieroglyphs being sometimes incised. The fine limestone of the Theban hills afforded a good surface for painting on. When a flint or fossil occurred it was extracted, and the hole filled up with cement.

Inscriptions accompany the scenes, sometimes containing biographies, which have been of much importance in piecing together the history of Egypt.

Toys. Several children's playthings have been discovered during excavations. There are dolls of many sorts—from wooden and ivory ones of the XIth Dynasty with movable arms to the Roman rag doll. Some have still hair left on their heads, others show the holes where the hair had been inserted. One figure is jointed at the arms and legs, fixed on a stand, and, being worked with a string, simulates a man crushing corn. A crocodile with a movable jaw has also been found. Many balls have come to light. Some are of wood painted two colours in sections, others are of leather stuffed with rushes.

Trade. Foreign commerce was limited for the Egyptians by the fewness of their ports; but a considerable amount of trade was carried on by caravan. Among the objects imported from various countries were vases from Cyprus and Crete, seats, chariots, coffers, wines from Syria, &c., birds and fish (dried fish from Tyre), eye-salve from Syria, fruit, horses, and some domestic animals. The rareness of any trading expedition beyond Mediterranean waters is evidenced by the extreme importance attached to the expedition to the "Land of Punt" (*q.v.*) organized and sent out by Queen Ḥātshepsut, and afterwards recorded with many illustrations on the walls of her temple at Dêr el Baḥri. The objects desired and obtained were incense trees, incense, gold, ivory, precious woods (including ebony), eye-paint, dog-headed apes, long-tailed monkeys, greyhounds, and leopard skins. All these were obtained by barter, the Egyptian ships having brought daggers, battle-axes, and gay ornaments; though the record puts it more picturesquely, calling the objects obtained "tribute," and the articles brought for exchange "an offering put there for the goddess Hathor." Of home trade we are well informed by the pictures on tomb walls. Since everything in daily use was made in the country, the class of craftsmen and tradesmen was very large. But trade seems never to have developed beyond the ordinary bazaar marketing business such as one sees in any eastern town nowadays. There were no merchant princes, nor did any mere tradesman win his way to notice, though one or two of the professions enabled a man to climb the ladder of rank. Each trade had its chief, its master mason, or master shoe-maker, or master smith. According to a writer in the Anastasi Papyrus the lot of all craftsmen was a hard one, but the hardships he enumerates would seem to be merely the necessities of the conditions of their labour; for instance, the blacksmith's fingers are "as rugged as the crocodile," the barber has to "run from street to street seeking custom," the mason is "exposed to all the winds" while he builds, &c. The principal craftsmen represented on tomb walls are sculptors, painters, carpenters, masons, boat-builders, metal-workers, glass-blowers, potters, weavers, sandal-makers, and confectioners. There was in early times, and later among the poorer classes, no recognized medium of exchange, so that business was done by barter, and apparently, as at the present day, much haggling took place.

Trees, Sacred. So important a part do certain trees play in the religious cult, that some Egyptologists have accepted tree worship as a fact. We read of a very ancient sacred tree in the "great hall" at Heliopolis, on the leaves of which Thoth and Safekh write the names of the monarch to secure to him immortality; but here the tree is rather a symbol than an object of worship. The nearest approach to actual worship was under the Ptolemies, when every temple seems to have had its sacred tree. Ten kinds of trees are mentioned. (*See* PERSEA TREE, SYCOMORE and FLORA).

Triad. A cycle of three gods, arising from the fact of other deities being associated with the chief god of the place. It consisted frequently of the god, a goddess his wife, and their son. The most important triad was that of Thebes, which was worshipped in most of its temples. They were Amen, Mut his wife, and their son Khensu. The triad honoured at Memphis was Ptah, Sekhet, Im-hetep; that at Kom Ombo, Sebek, Hathor and Khensu.

Tuamāutef, or **Duamāutef**, one of the four funerary genii, the four children of Horus, who are so frequently represented standing upon a lotus flower. Tuamāutef has the head of a jackal. They are the four cardinal points, and preside over the four Canopic jars (*q.v.*).

Tum.

Tum. Also called Tmu, Atmu and Atum, was the chief of the gods of Annu (Heliopolis). He may be considered as an aspect of Rā, for he represents the night sun. He is called "creator of men"; "maker of the gods"; "self-created." The ancient city of Pithom took its name from the fact of there being a temple "pa" (lit. house) of Tum there. He is represented as a man wearing the double crown of Egypt.

Tut-ankh-Ámen. *Neb kheperu Ra*, Dynasty XVIII (who came to the throne as Tut-ankh-Áten), reigned by right of his wife Ankh-es-en-pa-Áten, 3rd daughter of Ámen-hetep IV (Akh-en-Áten) *q.v.* Little is known of his time beyond the magnificence of his tomb and the greatness of Ay, court Chamberlain and successor.

U

Uaḥ-áb-Rā. *Ḥāā-áb-Rā*, Dynasty XXVI., cir.

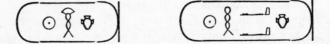

B.C. 591—572. The Apries of the Greeks, the Pharaoh Hophra of the Old Testament, who leagued unsuccessfully with Zedekiah against Nebuchadnezzar, king of Babylon. The Egyptian fleet, however, was successful against the Babylonian, and with its help Tyre held out against Nebuchadnezzar for thirteen years.

Hophra built a beautiful temple at Saïs, in the Delta. His soldiers revolted against him, shut him up in his own capital, and made Áāḥmes II., a man of low origin, but who had married the daughter of Psammetichus II., his successor.

Uast. The name for Thebes generally, and the capital of the fourth nome of Upper Egypt. Chief deity, Ámen Rā.

Ua-ua-t. A district of Ethiopia, east of Korosko.

Uazit. The tutelary goddess of the north, the Buto of the Greeks. She is represented wearing the crown of
Lower Egypt; but sometimes,
especially when figured with
Nekhebt, the goddess of the
south, she takes the form of a
winged uraeus, wearing the
same crown. Into her charge
Horus was given while Isis,
his mother, went to search for
Osiris.

Uazit.

Uer-mer. Name given to the sacred bull at Heliopolis, the Greek Mnevis (*q.v.*).

Unás. Very little is known of this
last king of the Vth Dynasty. His sepulchre, called
Nefer-àsu, i.e., "the most beautiful place," is the
smallest of the pyramids at Sakkâra, and lies to
the south-west of the Step Pyramid. The walls lining
the sarcophagus chamber are of alabaster and covered
with paintings, the colours of which are still fresh.
The fragments of the king's mummy were found
scattered on the floor.

"The decoration occupies only the end wall of the
funeral chamber; the part against the sarcophagus
was lined with alabaster, and engraved to represent
a great monumental door, etc."

Un-nefer. One of the names of Osiris. As Un-nefer
he is god and judge of the dead in the underworld.
The name signifies "the good being."

Uraeus. The snake (a species of cobra di capello)
seen always on the head-dress of the Pharaohs. It
was the symbol of royalty. (*See* ĀRAR and UAZIT.)

Ur ḥekâ. The instrument used in the funeral ceremonies for symbolically opening the eyes of the mummy.

User. A sceptre with greyhound (?) head found almost always in the hands of the gods. It is symbolical of power.

User-ka-f.  The first king of

Dynasty V., cir. 3721 B.C., reigned twenty-eight years.

Usertsen I., *Kheper-ka-Rā.* Second king of Dynasty

XII., cir. 2758 B.C., reigned forty-four years, perhaps longer. Carried on building works throughout Egypt. At Begig, in the Fayûm, lies a red granite obelisk of this reign which is unique, as it differs in shape from all other obelisks as yet found.

In the tomb of Âmeni at Beni Ḥasan, we have an admirable picture of the life of one of the great hereditary nobles of this period.

Usertsen II. *Khā-kheper-Rā.* Fourth king of

Dynasty XII., cir. 2684 B.C. A queen, Nefert, and three daughters are known.

The pyramid of Illahûn, at the entrance to the Fayûm, marks the burial place of this Pharaoh. The workmen's town lay a mile to the east; and was completely excavated by Petrie, who published plans of both streets and houses.

Usertsen III., *Khā-kau-Rā*, fifth king of Dy-

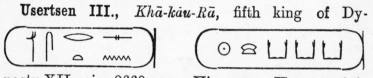

nasty XII., cir. 2660 B.C. His queen, Henut-taui, is known from her sandstone sarcophagus in the N. pyramid at Dahshur. It was in this pyramid that de Morgan found in 1894 the beautiful jewellery of the Princess Set-Hathor, probably a sister of Usertsen III.

This Pharaoh, according to a tablet at Sehêl, first cataract, ordered a channel to be made through the cataract, 34 ft. wide and 24 ft. deep, preparatory to the conquest of Nubia. At Semneh and Kummeh, about thirty miles south of the cataract, are two fortifications erected by Usertsen III., for the protection of his southern frontier against the Nubians.

Ushabtiu. The name given to figurines in the form of a mummy deposited with the dead. Their business was to act as the servants of the deceased in the underworld. The 6th chapter of the "Book of the Dead" is usually inscribed on them, and runs thus :—

" O *Ushabtiu*, if the Osiris (deceased) is commanded to do any work whatsoever in the *neter khert* let all obstructions be cast down from before him."

" Here am I, ready whensoever ye call."

" Be ye ready always to plough and sow the fields, to fill the canals with water, and to carry sand from the east to the west."

" Again, here am I when ye call."

Uten. ⊂⊃ A measure of value, or standard of exchange, more recently translated *tabnu*. It consisted of a piece of copper (?) wire, weighing from 91 to 92 grammes. So uniform was its weight that it was also used in the scales *as* a weight. The uten was only a standard, the piece itself did not necessarily change hands in transactions. (*See* MONEY.)

Uzat. *See* EYE, THE SACRED.

V

Veterinary Art. From various tomb-paintings, with their inscriptions, it has been found that the Egyptians were in the habit of doctoring their animals. One painting represents a man forcing a bolus, which he has taken out of a vase in front of him, down the throat of an ox, the inscription above reads, " doctoring a young ox." Careful examination of the left humerus of a mummied ibis, fractured and reunited in a particular way, convinced the learned Cuvier that it had undergone surgical treatment.

Vine. Throughout the country vines were grown from the Delta to Nubia. We are told (Harris papyrus) that Ramses III. planted numerous vineyards in the northern and southern oases as well as others, having ponds with lotus flowers. Another papyrus speaks of a celebrated mountain vineyard which belonged to the Temple of Amen at Thebes. The vine, as pictured on tomb walls, was trained over trellises, which were supported either by wooden pillars or, more simply, by wooden forks. (*See* WINE.)

Vulture. This bird was the symbol of maternity, and as such is sacred to Mut, the second in the divine triad of Thebes. The vulture is the ideographic hieroglyph, for her name has the value of *mut*. Many goddesses wear for head-dress a kind of cap in the form of a vulture. The goddess Nekhebt is sometimes represented in the form of a vulture.

W

Weapons. Stone weapons belonging to the early period have been recovered. They are of a light-brown flint. Besides bows and arrows, the Egyptians used different kinds of spears, javelins, slings, short swords, daggers and knives, battle-axes and clubs. Spears were made of a shaft of wood from five to six feet in length. The heads, fitted at the end into a metal band, were of bronze, and of various shapes. Javelins also had wooden shafts. Swords were short, straight, and sharp-pointed. The handles of daggers sometimes took the shape of hawk-heads, or are inlaid. (*See* Bow and ARROWS.)

Weaving. This industry, which was carried on by women, was brought to great perfection. Linen as fine as silk muslin was woven, and the Egyptians were very proud of their skill in its manufacture. The goddesses Isis and Nephthys wove garments for their husband and brother Osiris, and Neith bears for her symbol a shuttle on her head. Two kinds of looms are depicted on tomb walls; the earlier and simpler form at Beni Hasan, the later one at Thebes. (*See* LINEN.)

Wigs. Artificial head-dresses for both men and women were always in use. Apparently men shaved their heads, and for full-dress occasions put on a wig. Two kinds are distinguished on the monuments, the one short and imitating curly hair, and the other long. The details and arrangements of them vary at different periods and according to current fashions, but the two kinds always prevailed.

The ladies' wigs were invariably long, though the fashion of the coiffure changed continually.

They were usually made of human hair mixed with sheep's wool.

Wine. A favourite drink among the Egyptians. Four sorts were in use under the Old Empire, e.g. red, white, black, and northern wine. This last answered to the Mareotic wine, which was considered the best. Under the New Empire several kinds were often mixed together. When made the wine was stored in carefully stoppered jars and sealed by the "treasurer." Pictures of the making of wine may be seen on tomb walls. The men are depicted treading the wine-press, from which the wine runs out at the bottom; other men put it in amphorae and the treasurer seals them. A curious scene of mixing wines shows three siphons in separate jars being brought down to one large one. (*See* VINE.)

Winged Disk, The. *See* HOR BEHUTET.

Wool was to a certain extent considered impure, and hence was never used for burial wrappings; exceptions, in the case of some workmen's bodies, have been found at Tourah. For this reason the priests did not wear it next their skin; and always removed their outer woollen garment before entering the temple. Only the poor made much use of woollen garments. But, that wool was one of the chief articles of commerce is certain from the fact that large flocks of sheep were reared in the Thebaïd, where, according to Strabo, mutton was unlawful food. Each sheep yielded two fleeces in the year. An exception to the rule that wool was regarded as impure is the case of the two women who were to recite the "Festival songs of Isis and Nephthys" (*q.v.*). The directions in the papyrus are that they were to wear garlands of ram's wool.

X

Xerxes. *See* PERSIANS.

Xois, or **Chois.** The Greek name for *Chasuut,* the capital of the sixth nome of Lower Egypt, the modern Sakha. Chief deity, Åmen Rā.

Y

Year. (*a*) The Civil or Vague year consisted of twelve months, each of thirty days, to which were added five intercalary days at the close. These months were divided into the three seasons of Shet, inundation, Pert, growing, and Shat, sowing. The 20th July, which was about the beginning of the Nile rise, was looked upon as New Year's Day.

(*b*) The Sothic year of $365\frac{1}{4}$ days. This period was calculated by the rising of Sothis on the first day of the first month of Shat, when it coincided with the rise of the Nile.

(*c*) The solar year, which was to all intents and purposes the same as the Civil year.

Documents were dated from the day, month, and year of the reigning monarch. Professor H. Brugsch was of opinion that the " great year " corresponded to a lunar year with the addition of the intercalary days, and the " little year " to a lunar year, thus giving five different methods of reckoning the year.

Z

Zaān (the modern Sān; Greek, Tanis; and Hebrew, Zoan) is a kind of island in the swamp of the Delta on the branch of the river flowing into Lake Menzaleh, and is about twenty miles north of Tel-el-Kebir. The earliest local remains discovered are of the XIIth Dynasty; the few inscriptions bearing the name of Pepi-Meri-Rā being on blocks probably brought from Dendera and used here for the second time. Statues of Amen-em-hâts and Usertsens have been found; the temple, which was later enlarged and beautified by Ramses II., was the work of these monarchs. Most of the Hyksos antiquities which have been recovered came from Sān. They are all either of black or dark-grey granite.

A great feature of the temple precincts was a statue of Ramses II., which was between eighty and a hundred feet high, and was probably a monolith. Only fragments remain. Shashanq, of the XXIInd Dynasty, probably destroyed much of the work of Ramses, for his pylon is largely built of the fragments. To this day, Sān has served as a quarry for the neighbourhood.

Pasebkhānu, of the XXIst Dynasty, built an enormous wall enclosing the temple. It was eighty feet thick. Portions, twenty-five feet in height, still remain.

Under the XXVIth Dynasty, when Saïs became the capital of the Delta, the temple fell into disrepair. But houses were built in the shelter of the great wall during the XXIXth Dynasty, and Nectānebo II., of the XXXth Dynasty, sought its protection against the Persians. Three sphinxes of this period have been discovered.

Under the Ptolemies more houses were built. As

the area became filled up from the crumbling of the rain-washed walls, houses were built on the top of the wall, where a surer foundation was obtained. In Roman times they were built in the centre of the enclosure, the wall by that time being probably too far worn down to afford shelter, and too crumbling to be a suitable foundation. Sān was first excavated by Mariette. See vols. ii. and v. of publications of Egypt Exploration Fund. Book of Numbers, xiii. 22.

Zal, or **Zar**. Capital of *Khent-ábt*, the fourteenth nome of Lower Egypt. Horus was the divinity revered here.

Zerti. A term applied to Isis and Nephthys as protectors of the dead.

Zeser. Third king of Dynasty III. Reigned seven (?) years. The titles of this king occur in a rubric in the Turin Papyrus, and he is mentioned in a tale in the Westcar Papyrus. He is supposed to have built the Step Pyramid of Sakkâra.

Zodiac. The zodiacs found in Egypt are of late date. They have been found at Esneh, Dendera, and Contra-Lato. They were borrowed from the Greeks.